Social Media Marketing and Passive Income Mastery

A Complete Digital Advertising Guide Including Facebook, Instagram, Google SEO & Youtube! Best Ideas & Strategies to Make Money Online!

By Sean Buttle

"Social Media Marketing and Passive Income Mastery: A Complete Digital Advertising Guide Including Facebook, Instagram, Google SEO & Youtube! Best Ideas & Strategies to Make Money Online!" Written by "Sean Buttle".

Social Media Marketing and Passive Income Mastery is a bundle of the books "The Passive Income Guide to Financial Freedom", & "Social Media Marketing a Strategic Guide".

Hope You Enjoy!

The Passive Income Guide to Financial Freedom

Ideas and strategies to make money online through multiple income streams – affiliate marketing, blogging, dropshipping, network marketing and social media.

By Sean Buttle

Table of Contents

Introduction: What Exactly is the Passive Income Mindset?

There is a buzz about passive income all around us. Wherever you go, financial experts and wealth creation gurus are speaking about harnessing the power of passive income. What is this passive income and why is everyone focusing on creating multiple channels and sources of passive income? For that, first, do a reality check and answer a few questions.

Are you bucket carrier or pipeline builder? Bucket carriers work hard from 9-5 and carry buckets of water (money) back home. The water keeps coming as long as they go out there, work for a certain number of hours, and carry the buckets home.

However, there are some smart pipeline builders. Instead of carrying buckets each day, they build a pipeline of water so the water keeps coming to them even when they don't go out there to carry buckets. In traditional jobs and businesses, you are required to invest an "x" amount of time and effort to get paid in exchange for it. However, pipeline builders work just once to create their pipeline and enjoy an inexhaustible water supply for as long as they are alive.

This is exactly what passive income is about. It isn't about exchanging a fixed amount of time for fixed income. It is about creating streams of wealth that keep working for you long after you've stopped working. While bucket carriers work hard for their money, pipeline builders may their money work hard for them.

Have you ever noticed how some people have all the time in the world but no money to enjoy it (they are probably not working) while others have all the money in the world but no time to enjoy it (they are trading their time in exchange for all the money.) True financial freedom involves having all the money in the world along with all the time to enjoy it, which is possible only when you create reliable sources of passive income that keep making you money even while you are asleep.

Think about this – you have a bag of seeds. There are a few things you can do with them. Make a healthy crunchy snack out of it and relish it or plant them. Rather than eating the seeds immediately, you plant them. Once sowed, you nurture the seeds by watering it, protecting it from pests and use high-quality fertilizers. There are no noticeable results initially. You wonder if the time, effort, and money spent on nurturing these seeds are worth it. Despite being given the required care, they just take in everything and become invisible. However, you continue nurturing them for several days that go into weeks. Then the miracle occurs. A tiny seedling pops out. When you witness this, you feel motivated to keep going. You realize that if you continue feeding and watering the seeds, they will grow gradually but definitely. It may take several months or years. However, gradually the small, seemingly insignificant seed assumes the form of a fruit tree.

Even before you know it, the tree is filled with lots of delicious fruits. Now, instead of snacking on the seeds, your family can feast of the fruits coming from the thriving tree. Now, you plant more seeds that you get from the fruits. The process continues until you've built a huge orchard of fruit trees, which is more than sufficient to last you a lifetime.

This is the passive income mindset. Instead of spending money for the moment, you use it to create wealth for the future. The wealth that is able to give your family financial freedom.

Building passive income is about leveraging your efforts, time, and skills for making consistent income from it. For instance, let's assume you spend 60 hours conceptualizing, researching, writing, and marketing an eBook. You do all this once and keep earning a percentage of the sale price as royalty each time the book is sold for several years. Unlike traditional jobs and business, the income isn't proportionate to the time and effort invested. It has the potential to make you much more than what you've invested.

So even if you work for 60 hours, your earning potential is unlimited. You can make $600, $600 or even $6000 from the book because you are not exchanging a fixed amount of time for a fixed amount of money. The income is based on the number of copies you manage to sell for a product you spend time and energy creating just once. Instead of exchanging a fixed amount of time for wealth that is equal to those hours, you are smartly leveraging your time and energy by exchanging the fixed hours for income that can last you a lifetime.

Time is the most valuable commodity among all. Once lost, it can't be ever regained. Are you willing to exchange time for money? Do you want to lock your time for earning money in exchange for it? Each time you want to earn money, you'll have to trade time for it—valuable, precious and limited time. Wouldn't you want o to enjoy your time while building income streams that offer the potential of unlimited wealth by working for a limited period of time? If yes, it is high time you stopped carrying buckets and start building a pipeline.

Chapter One: Make a Killing With Self-Publishing

Self-publishing is one of the most lucrative ways of earning a passive income. All you need to do this create a product once and keep earning on it each time someone purchases it. Though the internet is crowded with multiple self-publishing platforms, Amazon Kindle probably offers the best self-publishing platform with its wide reach and popularity among eBook readers. It offers an easy to use, a potentially rewarding, and profitable platform for any aspiring author or internet entrepreneur looking to generate passive income through their books. eBooks sell far more than physical books on Amazon, which should be an indication of how it has revolutionized the online self-publishing domain.

The best about the entire deal is that you don't even have to be a known writer or personality to make it big on Kindle. All you need to do is follow Amazon's guidelines and create your own profitable eBook publishing empire.

Here is a handy step-by-step guide to building a profitable, rewarding and fulfilling virtual self-publishing business on Amazon Kindle.

1. Identify a popular and profitable niche

This is true for any virtual content-driven business. Find a middle spot between a topic where there isn't much competition and one with considerable demand. If you see a large number of books authored by "experts" or "authorities" in a particular domain, stay away from it. Similarly, avoid niches that are already crowded with too many titles. Look for sub-niches within wider niches.

For instance, if you find too many books on "how to enjoy a happy marriage or relationship", you may want to narrow it down to "how to communicate more effectively with your spouse/partner" or "how to tell if your spouse/partner is cheating in you" or "how to deal with a spouse/partner's infidelity" or "how to rebuild trust after your spouse/partner's affair" and other similar sub-niches or topics. You get the idea, right? Focus on some aspects of the wider niche then flesh it out. This sets your book apart from the rest (especially the tons of books on happy marriages in the above example) and also gives you a more focused audience (in the above case probably someone coping with adultery in their marriage). Go with a more focused and targeted topic if you find the Kindle marketplace already crowded with your niche. Trust me, there are still plenty of niches and sub-niches to tap into and explore, which makes it so stimulating.

One of the best tips to come up with best-selling topics is to identify desperate problems being faced by people around you. Create books that solve these desperate problems. It can range from getting rid of alcohol addiction to controlling one's anger to overcoming bad credit to divorce help. There are tons of problems for which people are looking for quick and effective solutions (ask someone who has acne or yeast infection how badly they want to cure it). Fill these gaps by creating an eBook around it. Books relate to hobbies also perform well on Kindle.

The fiction category is also fast picking up on Amazon Kindle, though non-fiction still remains ahead. If you are a more creatively inclined writer or can hire someone to write for you, create a fictional series by brainstorming plots, themes, genres, stories, and characters. Weave an engaging story around a popular theme or hire a ghostwriter to create it for you.

2. Research the demand and potential of your topic/niche

If you are planning to write a book that sells like hotcakes on Kindle, you better know its profit potential before beginning. Many new authors and eBook entrepreneurs create books passionately and then wonder why their books have no takers. More often than not, they choose books that aren't much in demand.

Start your research by typing the primary keyword for your book in the search bar. Ensure that the "All" filter is switched only to "Kindle Store." There will be a list of recommendations popping in the drop-down menu. These are the terms and phrases readers use while searching for titles on the Kindle marketplace, which should give you important clues about what exactly your target readers are actually looking for. This will tell you whether there is enough demand for your topic to create a book around it.

You can also look at the number of competing books while typing a keyword to help determine the competition in the categories and subcategories. For example, a topic such as "cure acne" could have a million books dedicated to it, considering the huge demand. However, if you narrow it down to "curing acne with ingredients available in your kitchen", you will have fewer competitors. It'll probably be easier to rank for the book within a sub-topic within the search option. Each time a reader looking for natural acne remedies searches for books related to the sub-topic, your book will pop up. If you simply write a broader book about acne remedies, it will probably be hidden under a ton of other books.

Look at top-selling books within a category or subcategory. What are the things that work for them? Have they left out important gaps that you can fill? Can you do something to beat them in their ranking? Go through the book's cover, title and sub-title, cost, description (very important), reviews, table of contents and preview pages (you can see these for some books), and rank. Let us say a book has 60 plus reviews and is a consistently top-ranking performer within the category or subcategory, it may be tough to beat it. It has already established itself as an ace product, and unless you can come up with totally path breathing that hasn't been covered by the book, you are better off going with another topic or niche.

3. Create a stunning and relevant eBook cover

Unfortunately, the "don't judge a book by its cover" adage doesn't work on Kindle. Books are often picked up solely based on their cover and description in the absence of any other information about its contents. eBook covers are probably one of the biggest factors affecting people's buying decisions. Make your cover relevant, attention-grabbing and attractive. Let it speak to your readers, and convey the essence of your book.

You could either create the cover yourself using software such as Photoshop (or anything similar) if you are aesthetically or graphically inclined. If not, you can outsource the task to a professional graphic designer on platforms as Fiverr or Upwork. Check their ratings and previous work if possible before hiring a graphic designer to do your eBook.

4. Write the book

Now that everything else is in place, you'll have to get down to work. Write the eBook yourself or hire a professional freelance ghostwriter to do the job for you for a fee while retaining the full rights of your book as the author/creator. Creating an eBook isn't as intimidating or time-consuming as it appears. For example, a book that retails for under $3 can be a 30-50 page creation. Concentrate on creating high-quality titles that wow readers with value rather than a 100 plus page junk that no one appreciates. As long as the book is able to offer clear solutions and a strong value proposition, readers aren't concerned with the number of pages.

Low-quality books will hurt your ratings, reviews, rank, and eventually your reputation as an author. Create a credible and authoritative reputation as a writer if you want to make a steady income as a self-publisher on Amazon Kindle. Focus on getting positive reviews by offering solid, real value to your readers. Ensure you stick to the Amazon Kindle formatting guidelines before publishing the book.

5. Publish it

Once you've followed all the formatting guidelines given by Amazon, make a KDP (Kindle Direct Publishing) account. Look for the "Bookshelf" option. Click "Add New Title" and go step-by-step according to the instructions mentioned.

Fill details such as the title, description, author name, and click the access to the next page. Add appropriate categories, subcategories, and keywords to make it easier for readers to access your book.

Authenticate your publishing rights. Then, upload the book cover along with your content file. There are simple and straightforward instructions for uploading your file, which can be followed even by beginners.

One of the areas where I've identified a clear gap (and which is an extremely crucial attribute) is book descriptions. Plenty of authors writer wow books but completely overlook creating an impactful description. Ensure you spend time and effort or shinning up your description and keep in the mind that the book should be as amazing as the description says it is or you'll end up with a lot of flak in the reviews.

Some authors or publishing entrepreneurs who don't want to reveal their identity write/publish books under a pen name.

As a kindle direct publishing author, you will have to pick your royalty option and publishing territory. You can choose the selling price of your book, along with setting royalty preferences. If your book's price is set below $9.99, you can bag 70% royalty on it. Also, if the book is lower than 3 megabytes, the lowest price to sell it for earning a 35% royalty is $0.99 while the highest is $200. For books that range from 3-10 megabytes and more than 10 megabytes, the least price for earning a 35% royalty is $1.99 and $2.99 respectively.

You can start by pricing your eBooks at 0.99 with a 35% royalty preference to get some early bird reviews that help rank your book. Once you bag some favorable reviews and ranks well for the main keywords, increase the price to $2.99 and go with the 70% royalty plan.

6. Master the review drill

Let me ask you something? How do you decide whether you want to buy something online without knowing much about the product or service? You seek validation for your purchasing decisions based on other users' experience with it. If a book has consistently earned low ratings, as a reader you are less likely to purchase it. Reviews are game-changers when it comes to determining the fate of your book.

Go through Amazon's Review Guidelines carefully to understand how the process works. One way to bag a lot of reviews is to virtually distribute free copies to influencers or authorities within your industry or domain and request them to write reviews. Look for these thought leaders and influencers within forums, dedicated communities, eBook review exchange groups, and social media channels. There are several groups and communities on Facebook and other channels where authors exchange books for reviews.

Stay away from false and paid reviews. Ensure you create high-quality eBooks that encourage people to leave behind flattering reviews than expecting them to falsely praise a crappy book. Influencers and thought leaders especially will offer unbiased reviews. If you intend to stay in the business for long, it is in your best interest to create valuable and high-quality titles.

7. Slay with the right promotion and marketing strategies

There are several ways to market your book on various platforms across the web, which only needs some amount of out of the box thinking. Register for the KDP Select Program for making more money on the Kindle Reader's Leading Library. There are several other benefits too such as complimentary promotions and deals. For being a part of the Select program, your book has to be exclusively published on the Kindle platform for a period of 90 days. This strategy may help the book rank faster and eventually bag a higher number of sales. Ensure you go through all the updated policies and options to make the right decision based on your sales and marketing objectives.

There is another important benefit of being a part of KDP Select. You can hand over complimentary book copies for a period of five days (any five days of your choice) spread over three months or even consecutively. While the promotion is on over a period of five days or a single day, your book will show under Amazon's free books. This can significantly boost your marketing and promotional strategies.

Then there are Countdown Deals that allow you to give buyers a fixed discount, which allows you to get some early attention and advantage for generating fast sales (and reviews). This, in turn, boosts your sales profile in the long run. All this is possible only through the KDP Select program.

Another promotion hack is to submit the eBook complimentary while the KDP Select promo is running on platforms such as Goodreads. You'll get plenty of additional downloads and exposure based on the topic and demand.

One of the best mediums for promoting your book is social media. Create an unmistakable buzz around the books across multiple social media platforms such as Twitter, Instagram, Facebook, YouTube, LinkedIn, and others. The thing about Amazon is, it will promote your eBook only if the book generates some initial sales, which means you will have to create some early effort to make a few sales before Amazon can push it further for you.

Power-Packed Strategies for Social Media Marketing

1. Host an interesting and engaging Twitter party. Self-publishing entrepreneurs and writers adore Twitter since it's a fun, engaging and interactive platform for peddling your book without resorting to aggressive sales strategies. Host giveaway contests or launch party to start your online promotional drive. I recommend coming up with a catchy, memorable, and unique hashtag for the party. Tweet a few teasers from the eBook. Organize a live question and answer session to add value to your interaction with your target audience.

2. Build a page, community, or group devoted to a topic related to the book on Facebook, and post informational content about it regularly in the run-up to the book launch. If you offer valuable content, connect with your potential readers and make an

effort to offer actionable solutions, they may lap up your book faster than you can imagine.

3. A popular social media promotion strategy used by many bestselling authors involves tweeting interesting snippets from their books. Remember, social media platforms aren't the right place for telling your potential readers to "buy your book right away." Avoid using it as a hard-selling medium. Instead, use it to build a connection with your readers, while also establishing your authority, credibility, and expertise as an author or thought influencer. It is the soft selling platform that should be used to build a reputation and loyal following. The authors will do well to use the social for their brand-building efforts. Build trust by offering high value and interesting content, which will invariably help your eBook sales soar.

4. While plenty of authors turn to Twitter and Facebook for promoting their books, LinkedIn remains an unexplored option for creating a buzz around these books. The strategy can be even more effective when it comes to eBooks related to business and management. List the books you've authored under the publication options of your LinkedIn profile. Start a discussion around the topic by creating a focused discussion group. Another strategy involves including

the book's name within the summary. Anyone scanning your profile can see it. This also establishes your expertise in a specific domain. Don't ignore the updates section, where you can include quotes, important lines, snippets and other extracts from the book.

5. Pinterest is another interesting and unexplored platform that can be used to promote your books in a visually arresting and aesthetically appealing manner. There are tons of resourceful ideas to create hype around your book on Pinterest. Start by making a pinboard of books that inspired you to write a book about the topic or that you used for your research. Use quotes connected to the topic of your book. You can also use visuals related to the niche or topic that inspires you. Some authors also create a visually stunning pinboard of pictures from their books.

If you want to go a step ahead, I'd suggest hiring the services of a professional graphic artist to make an infographic related to your eBook. If you don't want to increase your costs, create an infographic yourself using a platform such as Canva or Infogram. Infographics make for one of the most share-worthy content formats on social media. Ensure that you use your own pictures or royalty-free images that don't get you into copyright infringement issues. Include lines from your books on these photographs to make them even more impactful. Make several of these and add them on a dedicated pinboard.

Chapter Two: Making Your Way Into The Passive Income Club With Youtube Videos

As per an article in Forbes, the planets highest-earning Youtuber (Pewdipie) earns a hefty $12 million/year only through YouTube videos. This can give you an idea about the platform's potential when it comes to making passive income. YouTube is an engaging, versatile, and creative platform for creating video content that is instantly lapped up by viewers. The textual content has become more or less passé. Pressed for time and looking for instant gratification, people enjoy watching different types of videos. An online entrepreneur serious about building a steady stream of passive income can create lots of educational, informative and entertaining content to wow viewers. You can create videos on just about anything from making the perfect pizza to growing a home vegetable garden to spoofs of your favorite films. The platform is as flexible, multi-genre and resourceful as you want it to be.

Those with talents, specific skills, or passion for entertaining people can make a real killing by creating highly engaging and original YouTube videos.

A step-by-step guide to getting started with earning revenue as a YouTuber.

1. Make a YouTube account and channel

Before you begin your association with YouTube, ensure you go through their community guidelines. It is pretty exhaustive and keeps changing periodically so it's best to go through before starting. This will ensure your video content is compatible with the medium's policies.

You can create a YouTube account with your Gmail or Google login details. Once done, the user is directed to YouTube's homepage. Every user is given a channel by default, which is associated with their account. It's best though to create a new channel and keep your Gmail/Google account distinct from your YouTube channel. It'll make things easier and more streamlined.

Create your YouTube Channel

- Click on the Sign-In option in the top right corner of the YouTube homepage.

- You can either log in with your existing Google account or create a new one exclusively for YouTube. I'd recommend creating a new one but if you want to go with an existing account, that's also fine.
- Look for the profile picture icon on the top right, and click on the "Settings" icon.
- Under settings, pick the "create a channel" option.
- You can create a personal channel using your own name or use the name of your brand/business. Plenty of YouTubers give creative names to their channel to make it more appealing and entertaining. Pick a name according to your content genre and objectives and choose the right category. You'll access YouTube as a channel now. Put on your creative hat and add an eye-catching logo. Use attractive graphics to grab the viewer's attention and convey the gist of your content or channel theme. Add an email that you can use for receiving business-related queries.

2. Create compelling and addictive video content

If you want to make it big on YouTube or use it as a reliable source of passive income, in the long run, you better create awesome video content. There is no shortcut to success. If you want something you've never had, you've got to be prepared to do something you never did before. As simple as that! You can't keep doing the same things expecting different results.

Create wow-worthy and high-quality videos that grab plenty of eyeballs and help you build a loyal following of viewers. Concentrate on creating a large viewer base by creating and sharing videos that have the potential to go viral. It isn't easy but it isn't impossible either. In the *Contagious: Why Things Catch On* author Johan Berger mentions how people tend to share content that increases their social currency, social worth or makes them smarter among their social connections.

Create content about whatever you are good at and make a killing at it. It can be anything from satire to rap songs to mimicking popular artists. There are lots of scopes, and still, plenty of genres left untapped. If your content complies with the platform's guidelines, go ahead and create awesome videos around it. Look at the top videos on YouTube for inspiration just to know the type of content that fares well. Shoot engaging and high-quality videos with top-notch sound quality that generate lots of views.

Keep in mind the fact that internet users have a short span of attention. They are looking for quick information, solutions, and gratification. If something doesn't appeal to them, they'll quickly move on to another source. Keeps your video content appealing enough for them to stick with it by making a favorable first impression. It may sound ruthless but you have only a few seconds to make a stunning first impression. If you're opening and follow-up content isn't good enough, you won't be able to build the required interest.

3. Focus on gaining a massive number of subscribers

Getting a large number of viewers is important for raking in money on YouTube. The larger the number of video views you garner, the higher will be your income. You'll enjoy a higher subscriber base, who will ascertain repeat views for videos you make in the future.

Incorporate the right keywords for the title and description for ensuring they show up on search engines when users are actively seeking content related to your content topic or niche. You want the videos to be easily found by your target audience. The videos can be promoted on social media channels such as Facebook, Instagram, and Twitter. There is a feature for embedding your YouTube videos within your blog.

Write informative, useful, and engaging articles related to the videos for making your content more comprehensive and in-depth. One of the best ways to rank on search engines is to create diverse and versatile content like videos, images, and well-written text. Search engines instantly take to content that is in-depth and presented in multiple formats.

4. Earn revenue with AdSense

Now we talk about how does one make money with YouTube? Advertisements can be embedded within the video for earning neat profits from it. Visit the "Video Manager" option and select monetization. Your channel will have to go through a monetization approval process. Link your channel to Google AdSense for earning in advertisement revenue. Here's how you can connect the channel to your Google AdSense account:

- Log-in to YouTube

- Click on the "enable monetization" option by going to channel settings and selecting monetization.
- Go to the next screen and accept all the terms and conditions to submit.
- Click on the "Link my account" option just above the "almost there" message. Key in details related to your AdSense account or creates a brand new one. If you create an altogether new account, you may have to wait until it gets approved. The monetization process can begin immediately after the account is approved.
- For creating monetization only for specific videos, click on the "video manage" tab. You'll see "$" sign next to videos that are eligible for monetization. Click on this option and visit "video settings" where you can access the "monetize with ads" feature. Copyrighted videos always a notice displayed next to the video. The original owner of a piece of content can claim video rights even if the video has been uploaded by another person. If someone is trying to claim copyrights over content created by you, you can dispute it.

Pretty much like other online monetization methods, earning money through AdSense on YouTube requires creating a loyal viewership that loves your content and eagerly await your videos. Don't focus simply on filling your videos with tons of advertisements. New users who haven't yet been exposed to your content won't take too kindly to it. Build a loyal following first by offering useful and engaging content before you decide to monetize your channel.

The key to making passive income online is offering real value to your users before you can hope to earn from them. AdSense may not approve your monetization request based on the fact that you may not have enough followers. Hence, in the beginning, focus on building a steady stream of loyal viewers, followed by monetizing your channel. Create content that is unique and stands out. Offer incredible value to your subscribers, and don't forget to optimize these videos so they are easily found during searches. How does one keep track pm viewer statistics? Access all your statistics from the YouTube Analytics page.

5. Utilize affiliate marketing monetization methods
Affiliate marketing is another wonderful way to monetize your YouTube content. There are plenty of

informational products, real products, applications and services that can be promoted through your YouTube videos. Include an affiliate link in the description section.

Every time viewers use your unique affiliate link to buy a product/service, you'll earn a commission. Affiliate marketing is known to generate higher income than advertisements on YouTube. Use this monetization method cleverly to make the most of your channel. Ensure the products or services you are promoting through your affiliate links are related to your video and of interest or value to your target subscribers. You don't want to push a bunch of turkeys that lead to a loss of subscribers and credibility. Stick to high-quality, relevant and value-adding products and services that help make the purchasing decision easy for your buyers.

For instance, if you are creating a recipe or food videos, you can include links of the platform or marketplace from where your audience can buy cookware that you've used in your video. In this manner, people who are interested in following your recipes will know where to source high-quality cookware from.

6. Create videos to direct traffic to your blog

Engaging, informative, and interesting videos are a great way to channelize traffic towards your blog. Use your blog link within the video's description section. Urge visitors to act by clicking on the blog link. This YouTube can be used for making money through ads and affiliate offers on the niche blog.

7. Utilize the YouTube partner program

Once your channel gains popularity and you bag plenty of views, you can qualify for the YouTube partner program, which is a popular way of earning additional income. Also, brands may approach you to sponsor your content or create videos for promoting their products and services in exchange for a fee.

However, you need to establish yourself as an influencer or authority within your domain before brands can approach you. You have to be a thought leader or community influencer to get people to buy through your suggestions and recommendations for brands to approach you and pay you a hefty endorsement fee. However, plenty of YouTubers are making money through sponsored videos and brand associations.

For the YouTube partner program, there is no clearly laid out eligibility conditions. At times, some channels get approved even with 100 (or less than 100) subscribers. One of the biggest benefits of being approved for the YouTube partner program is you'll get to use plenty of advanced and sophisticated tools for boosting your content, thus helping you garner even more subscribers. This translates into increased exposure, higher views, and eventually greater profits. The partner program is worth considering if you want to increase your YouTube earnings or are serious about using it as a reliable source of passive income.

8. Tips for growing your YouTube subscribers

- Use awesome titles for your videos. Keep the titles pithy, compelling, and brief. It should be intriguing enough to arouse the viewer's interest. For example, if the video is about a cat eating pasta, give it a catchy title such as "Cat Pasta Mess." Don't reveal too much. All the same, stimulate the viewer's attention and interest.
- Plenty of YouTubers use the Clickbait strategy for enticing their readers to click on a link by drafting impossible to ignore headlines. You have seen plenty of headlines such as, "You won't believe the comeback of this bird after

being chased by a dog." The viewer obviously wants to find what extraordinary feat, action, or reaction was performed by the bird, which compels them to watch the video. Use your primary or most relevant keywords in the title organically for optimizing these videos for popular search engines. However, if you are using Clickbait, ensure it delivers what you promise in the headline. Otherwise, viewers will stop trusting you and watching your videos.

- Describe your videos accurately and in a detailed manner. Draft a few paragraphs describing the contents of the video in brief. Optimize your video content by incorporating the right keywords.

- Promote your content on platforms such as Google Plus, Facebook, Twitter, Pinterest, and other social media platforms. Get people to act like, comment, as well as share your videos. Give your videos the much-needed exposure. Connect your account with other social media platforms like Google Plus. Use applications such as ifttt.com to automate the process of posting on multiple social media platforms.

- Use tags for more effective optimization. Incorporate all-important keywords in the video's titles and descriptions in the "tags" to gather higher viewership. Use appropriate, relevant, and suitable tags for boosting the exposure of your video while viewers look for it. These tags are similar to hashtags used on Twitter and Instagram.

- Let's say, for instance, you are creating a video of a kitten playing with a puppy, you could come up with several tags such as "cute puppy kitten play" or "kitten puppy love." Don't use additional words that people don't include in their searches while utilizing tags that are popular on videos in multiple categories.
- End each video with a call for action. Every video should ideally have you urging the viewers to take action. People are likelier to take action when you make things simpler for them by telling them exactly what you want them to do. Don't assume that your viewers will automatically know what to do. Say something like, "Hit the like button now; it doesn't take more than a few seconds." At times, people may enjoy a video but not notice the share buttons. Remind them to like and share content to increase engagement and shares.

- Another expert tip to gather a lot of likes, shares, and comments is to mention something that people have a solid opinion on, which will get to share and interact.
- Ask them to comment on their views about something. Urge them to share their opinion in the comments section. For example, you may upload a travel video of animals giving tourists joyrides in international sanctuaries and ask people for their opinion on it. Pose insight questions towards the end to gain traction from seemingly controversial, debatable, and opinionated topics.
- Create playlists. YouTube playlists aren't very different from your regular playlists. They serve the same objective. It is easier for viewers to watch other videos by you when you create a playlist. Easy access is the key to increase viewership and exposure on the internet. When you present things in an easier to access and digest format, people will watch/read it.

Anything that is time-consuming or takes a lot of effort stands of higher chances of being rejected. People are looking for quick consumption of information and entertainment. Don't make potential viewers think too much or run around the place if you want a loyal viewership.

Proven Strategies for Creating Revenue-Earning YouTube Videos

Making YouTube videos can be a wonderful way of making money if you know what type of content is popular and easily lapped up by viewers. Your channel has the potential to offer plenty of influencer traction to gain a high number of subscribers. The area where most newbie online entrepreneurs struggle is coming up with ideas for money-making niches. They aren't able to come up with inspiring and attention-grabbing ideas. It is challenging to zero down on a popular niche that is lapped up by viewers.

Here are a few ideas for creating money-making YouTube video niches:

- Cooking videos are a rage on YouTube and predictably so. Everyone is eager to whip up new culinary creations and wants an easy, step-by-step instructional tutorial for the same. Viewers can keep going back over to the recipes each time they desire to cook something or miss a few steps, which makes it an incredible platform for recipe tutorials. Food is also an insanely visual medium that offers plenty of scope for creativity, presentation, and innovation. One tip to the lower competition is to narrow down your channel niche. For example, if the cooking niche is too crowded, go with something narrower such as healthy kids' lunchbox recipes or 10-minute breakfast recipes.

This can help you dominate the breakfast cooking or kids' lunchbox sub-niche. It can also be anything from one-pot meals to diet smoothies. This will help people searching for your narrower sub-niches find your channel, thus making it more focused. Make high-quality videos for traditional, exotic, or simple recipes and watch your viewership increase! Keep it too broad and you may not find plenty of takers unless you are an already established personality in the cookery domain.

- Then there is the hugely popular food adventure niche that involves creating videos of your food adventures at different places across the city, country, or world. Some videos of Indian street treats have earned a whopping 2.2 million views in a few months. So you can imagine the scope of the genre. Record your food adventures everywhere if you are a foodie or enjoy dining at different places.

- Another popular genre is product unboxing videos. If you've bought a beauty product, toy, unique product (that has a lot of curiosity or buzz surrounding it), or subscribe to one of the latest fads (beauty boxes based on monthly subscriptions), it can be a solid moneymaker for you. Offer unbiased and objective reviews of these subscription boxes or products by creating unboxing videos to show viewers exactly what they can expect from it. If you find something truly valuable or useful, mention it to viewers. Ensure you mention the not so flattering aspects of the products/services too to help your viewers make the right purchasing decision.

- One niche that is soaring in popularity and is fairly evergreen is the gadget review niche. Plenty of YouTubers are raking in steady passive income each month by creating insightful, informative, unbiased, and in-depth reviews of the latest smartphones, tabs, and other gadgets. The advertising revenue will end up paying for your gadget purchases if you have a steady number of followers plus you may make some additional profits, too. Much like other businesses, it will require time, effort, and resourceful thinking on your part. Review and rate the latest or newly launched devices. Once you establish yourself an influencer in the tech domain and have people seeking your recommendations/suggestions, tech companies may approach you to promote/review their products in exchange for a nice fee.

- Prank and prank fail videos are also extremely popular on YouTube nowadays and don't require much other than a creative mind. Videos that are high on humor have the potential to go viral immediately. Record videos of playing pranks on friends, partners, and family members! Grab their natural reactions. Learn slick editing and add more professional effects to make the videos even more attention-grabbing.

- Spycams are available all over the internet. The bo9lder lot can also attempt to prank strangers. Street magic and other magic trick videos are gathering plenty of traction on YouTube. Share a few magic tricks and pranks with your viewers to help them become popular among their friends.

- Prank fails are also gaining popularity of YouTube and have plenty of laugh value and preposterousness attached to it. It isn't something that usually happens, which makes it grab plenty of eyeballs when it does. Create prank fail scripts that look genuine, and make your viewers sit up and take note.

- Book reviews are hugely popular on YouTube. Avid readers often scan through video reviews of books they plan to read to know if it is worth the time and effort. Similarly, a review of movies and television series are also popular. Ensure to include book reviews of popular books, films, and Netflix series that people are looking to know more about. Make compelling videos about books and movies without revealing minute details of the plot. Insightful and analytic details of the book/series or a critique of the same are much sought after. Incorporate some famous quotes and lines from the book to make it more impactful and interest-arousing.

- How to videos tutorials are hugely popular on YouTube. Viewers are always for looking for craft, hobby, and other DIY videos or hacks. Learn new skills, art, and hacks to make popular videos around it. "How to" isn't really a niche but more of content type for the format that can help viewers learn everything from how to play the guitar to how to fix a flat tire to how to remove stubborn stains from your clothes. Make your video easy to understand, step-by-step, and useful. It should offer a clear value to your viewers if you want to make it more share-worthy. Search engine optimization and other internet marketing tutorials also perform well on YouTube because newbie marketers are almost always looking for different ways to make money online by learning the tricks of the trade from experts.

- Screen casting is also a popular YouTube activity to help you record screen activity on a computer or electronic device as it is happening. This gives you the scope for creating multiple web, gadget, and computer-based applications by recording your screen activity while actually doing these tasks. Offer people a resolution for common technical snags or teach them how to use various applications more effectively. Share shortcuts and productivity hacks to fill your videos with utility and high value. Plenty of viewers are seeking fast solutions for their technical problems. This format is especially suitable for people who are camera shy and wish to stay behind the scenes while still making the most of their skills and technical knowledge. The channel can also double up as software, website, and application reviewing software.

- Then there are travel videos which have consistently remained on top of popularity charts for their visual appeal and informative content. Monetize your travel adventures by recording high-quality videos of it. Objective, unbiased first-hand experiences and reviews are always sought after by viewers planning to visit a destination. You can cover everything from places of tourist interest to food to local culture to shopping. Underwater adventure videos (snorkeling and scuba diving) are quite popular and so are cruise journeys road trips, and shopping trips. Keep your narrative unique, interesting, conversational and personal. Your target audience should be able to relate to your adventures.

- Stand up comedies, satire, spoof, mimicry, and other humor formats are also popular on YouTube. Your claim to fame can be doing a take-off on popular celebrities and international sensations. These videos have a massive share value, which means you can earn greater exposure and popularity. Often, these videos are shared and endorsed by the celebrities themselves on their social media accounts.

- Alternately, you can interview popular bloggers and YouTube sensations for hearing their success stories. Plenty of viewers are eager to know the behind the scenes story of a particular blog, website, or YouTube channel. Get these internet stars to share some of their insider tips and success stories and you'll have the audience eating out of your hands. It also helps the star bloggers and YouTube sensations present themselves as experts or influencers on multiple platforms while targeting a wider audience base.

- Some YouTubers have made a fortune out of sharing their take on controversial and hot current topics. It can be a spoof, satire, or sarcastic take on a topic that is gathering plenty of national or global attention. Where to find trending topics? Google Trends is the best place for hunting down currently popular, trending, and viral topics. Trending niches can gather lots of early views quickly if you do it right.

- The next popular category is for fitness and exercise videos. Lots of people are looking for quick and effective exercises that help them lose weight or lead a healthier lifestyle. You can also combine these fitness videos with fun dance routines, yoga, and meditation. Share diet plans that have worked for you, healthy recipes, easy to follow workout techniques, and reviews of weight loss supplements.

Ensure though that you don't offer any medical advice (if you are not qualified to offer it) and always recommend that your viewers consult their medical practitioner before they follow any diet plan or exercise/fitness routine. Think about partnering with qualified nutritionists, dieticians, gym trainers, and more to offer people more comprehensive and all-around fitness or weight loss solutions.

- Babies doing an impromptu dance or something equally cute are quite a rage on YouTube. Plus owing to the cuteness factor, they also garner plenty of likes, comments, and shares. Make these acts unique and they'll act as absolute de-stressors for your audience. People love to take a break from their stressful schedule and watch cute videos that make them laugh or happy. These videos are also widely circulated on family and social groups.

Irrespective of the type of content you are creating from the above list (or your own topic), it is important to build a connection with your viewers to keep them coming back for more. Build trust, authority, credibility, and expertise if you want them to look up to you for information or entertainment. Building a rapport or connection is a must for almost any online business. They will be wowed by your content but a favorable rapport will make them come back for more.

Chapter Three: Ruling Affiliate Marketing

Affiliate marketing is one of the best ways to sink your teeth into the world of online passive income generation. What makes it so lucrative for beginners is the fact that you don't need to create own products, services, courses or anything. While you learn to build your own products or content, you can reap rich profits by promoting other people's products and services in exchange for commissions or a percentage of the sale. Plenty of internet marketers are making a full time living out of affiliate marketing. Contrary to the popular perception that the industry is outdated or saturated, trends reveal that affiliate marketing is slated to grow into a $7 billion industry in the next five years. If you aren't cashing in on this wonder of a moneymaker, you are leaving a lot of money on the table for competitors.

Here's a heads up about affiliate marketing and the secret strategies that you can master to make a killing out of it.

Affiliate Marketing Demystified

Affiliate marketing is one of the oldest revenue-generating opportunities on the internet that has changed the lives of thousands of virtual entrepreneurs. How does affiliate marketing work? As an affiliate marketer, associate or partner, you simply sign up to promote other people's products or services and earn a percentage of the sale price each time someone purchases the product or takes some action related to it through your unique affiliate link (which is tracked by the merchant).

In other words, you are simply recommending or suggesting your readers buy products or services that you think are useful or valuable to them in some way and earn profits by making these valuable recommendations each time a sale comes through from your affiliate links. Commissions differ hugely and may range from $1 going all the way up to $10,000 depending on the product you've chosen to promote.

Think of affiliate marketing as similar to how property agents operate. They don't win properties that are up for rent or sale. Instead, they recommend, suggest or promote other people's properties to prospective buyers in exchange for a percentage of the property deal.

5 Reasons Why you should consider Affiliate Marketing as an Online Revenue Creation Model

1. You don't need a product or service

This one's a no-brainer and one of the top reasons why newbie internet entrepreneurs find affiliate marketing so lucrative. You don't need to build products, services, systems, and selling mechanisms from scratch. Everything is in place for you to start promoting and marketing other people's products and services right away. All the systems are pre-built for you to benefit from with minimal effort on reinventing the wheel or building a process from scratch. Instead, you can focus all your efforts on promotion and marketing.

I mean you really can't launch a blog and website and populate it with your products and services overnight. Creating your own products and services is a time consuming, investment heavy, and intensive task. You may not have the time, specialized skills, and money to invest in creating your own products or services. Affiliate marketing can be a savior in such instances.

2. Low start-up capital

Compare setting an affiliate marketing business vis-à-vis its returns with that of a conventional business. It doesn't swallow a huge straight-up capital investment only to give flimsy returns over a period of time. To launch a traditional business, you need everything from retail space to a ready inventory amounting to several hundred or thousand dollars to overhead expenses. On the contrary, an affiliate marketing business can be started at the price of a couple of meals.

3. No requirement of specialized knowledge or expertise

Of course, if you are an established authority in a domain, it will add to your power as an influence to get people to buy various products and services. However, you don't need any specialized knowledge or expertise to make a killing at affiliate marketing as a virtual business. For example, if you are promoting weight reduction supplements, you really don't have to be a qualified nutritionist.

All you need to do is give comprehensive, detailed, factual, and unbiased information to make your reviews genuine and compelling enough to encourage your readers to purchase the product through your link. Affiliate marketers need enthusiasm and eagerness for recommending suitable products and services to the relevant target audience.

4. A huge source of passive income

Affiliate marketing is an excellent method for learning passive income online. Think of it as earning income on a property you own. Your website is your real estate, and you can rent out different spaces on your website to affiliate marketing offers for earning steady commissions from them each month.

This passive revenue-earning can continue for as long as the property is owned by you. In a conventional job or business, you invest time and effort once and get paid for it once. The beauty of passive income thought is once you get a system up and running, you have the potential to get paid multiple times or a lifetime for doing something once or a few times. Money can be made literally while you are asleep for completing a task once.

5. Abundant location and professional independence

There's no doubt about it—you are your own boss. You have complete professional independence to determine everything from what type of products you wish to promote to your work hours to strategies for scaling up the business. As an online entrepreneur, you are completely in control of your business. So, yes those visuals of online marketers sitting on a faraway beach with an exotic tropical drink in their hands, while their bank account gets fatter overnight may not be so far-fetched after all.

Affiliate marketing is a flexible option that doesn't tie you down to a rigid schedule. You can start it as a secondary or supplementary source of income alongside a full-time job, and quit your day job once you begin to witness success by scaling it up. You have complete freedom to pick your work hours, work on the move, and lead a more geographically independent life.

How does the Affiliate Marketing Business Model Work?

As an affiliate marketer, you start by setting up your own blog or website. Of course, one can launch an affiliate marketing business without a blog or website but if you are serious about making it a steady and reliable source of income, in the long run, you'll eventually need a professional-looking blog or website. Owning a website or blog is similar to claiming ownership of virtual land or real estate, which can be monetized in the long run through multiple ventures, one of which is affiliate marketing. By launching a credible, authoritative and valuable resource for your target audience, you can look to reap steady long term profits from the website.

There are unique links referred to affiliate links for every product or service you intend to promote on your page. These come with built-in trackers and recorders that help the original product/service creating company or merchant to determine precisely who the sale has to be attributed to, which means each time a website user makes a purchase through your unique link, you are duly credited for it.

The merchant benefits because they get a wider exposure and audience base for their products or services. The customer benefits because he/she finds products or services that are valuable for them. The affiliate marketer benefits because they receive a commission in exchange for promoting someone else's products and services. Since it's a win-win for everyone involved, the business model of affiliate marketing is pretty strong and less likely to crumble like other turkey online business models.

As a website or blog owner, your objective is to increase your conversions or get as many readers or users to buy from your link as possible. The greater the number of folks clicking on these affiliate links, the higher are your opportunities of converting the clicks into sales commissions.

Affiliate marketing is undoubtedly a numbers game or game of averages. Acing it involves attracting a large amount of targeted traffic to your website or blog while enticing them to purchase through your affiliate link by offering valuable products or services, useful insights and comprehensive reviews that help them buy. Remember this very crucial point—you are guaranteed to fail if you approach affiliate marketing as simply selling a bunch of products or services to your customers. Instead, change the approach to helping them buy. Make it easier for them to choose products and services that are most useful and relevant for them through detailed reviews, unbiased recommendations, and comprehensive posts.

Build a steady flow of web traffic over a period of time because it's all about numbers at the end of the day. Only a small percentage of people who visit your website will click on your affiliate link. Then again, only a small percentage of those who click on your link will purchase form the link. Thus, the higher the number of users visiting your webpage, the higher will be your click-through rates and conversions. Increase your traffic through various traffic generation methods (mentioned later in the chapter) to earn more clicks, sales, and commissions.

Affiliate Marketing: Step-by-Step Process

Here's a step-by-step breakdown of how the affiliate marketing process works:

1. Select a niche

To launch your own affiliate marketing website or blog, you need to zero down on a lucrative niche or sub-niche that isn't too competitive enough to be saturated and too low on-demand to not have an audience or takers. Find a sweet spot between the two. You need a niche that is too crowded yet has considerable demand and interest among a targeted audience. Watch out for niches that solve a problem.

Evergreen niches include those related to health, wealth, and relationships since everyone is almost always looking for glowing health, ways to make money, and stay in fulfilling relationships. Dig these evergreen niches for plenty of sub-niches. Then again, niches related to hobbies, travel, food, and lifestyle also do well as they have an aspirational value attached to them.

When a niche is too broad or competitive, try narrowing it down to a sub-niche. This way you'll stand a chance of ranking well for or capturing a smaller sub-niche than being nowhere with a big niche. When it comes to affiliate marketing, it pays to be a big fish in a small pond rather than a small fish in an ocean. Identify and dominate a niche by narrowing it down. For example, a niche like weight loss is done to death. You'll stand a very low chance of dominating a niche as vast as this with several big players already vying for the top spot on weight loss searches. However, if you narrow it down to something like "post-pregnancy weight loss", you have higher chances of dominating a niche with laser targeted users (women who are looking to knock off the extra post-pregnancy pounds).

There's an eternal debate between goings with a niche you are passionate about versus a money-making niche. I'd say stay somewhere in between again. If you are looking to build a long term, steady and sustainable business, it won't survive much without an element of passion. To go through tedious hours of content creation and promotion, you will have to have some amount of interest in the subject. Then again, plain passion without results or demand will not help you pay the bills, which will be de-motivating enough to make you quit eventually. Passion should also bring in the money because let's face it—we are talking about building a source of passive income in the long run.

Think about a niche you are fairly interested in, and which also has considerable demand. You must enjoy researching, writing and promoting the topic you pick.

Also, it should have a nice range of affiliate marketing products and services to promote.

Find appropriate, valuable and relevant products and services to promote

Once you've zeroed down on a niche or topic, identify the products or services you wish to promote on your blog or website. There are plenty of affiliate networks and marketplaces where you can find products and services across multiple niche and categories. They'll also have the product's or service's performance statistics at your fingertips to determine if you want to promote the product. Pick products that are most suitable, relevant and appropriate for your target audience. For instance, if you have a website about money-saving tips, you can't promote luxury vacations.

Once you sign up as an affiliate for the selected products or services, the merchant will create your unique affiliate link, which can be used for promoting the products or services on multiple platforms.

2. Create a website

Though there are affiliate marketers doing business without a blog or website, a website will help you make the process more effective and streamlined. Don't be intimidated at the prospect of building a website. It isn't as scary as it seems. WordPress has tons of amazing templates, customization options, and plug-ins to help you build professional, easily navigable, user-friendly and awesome looking web pages with a few clicks. Gone are the days of tedious coding and programming, which makes it easier for a newbie to set up their own affiliate marketing venture.

3. Fill it with drool-worthy content

This is the backbone of your affiliate marketing business. Do not expect to build a shady webpage by throwing in a bunch of crappy affiliate marketing links; expect to make a fortune overnight. It doesn't work that way in the virtual world. You have to offer your readers real value first through high quality, authoritative, in-depth and valuable content before they trust you enough to buy based on your suggestions and recommendations. Establish a credible brand that gives readers value before earning from them.

For the first few months, avoid focusing on making money and simply concentrate on building a trustworthy, credible, and identifiable brand. Your audience should be able to identify with your brand

and connect with it. The content should resonate with your target audience, and make them sit and take notice. Create informative and sharable content.

It isn't just limited to textual content and blog posts anymore. There are multiple content formats that are gaining huge popularity on social media, such as videos and infographics. Give value to readers by making the content highly useful and engaging for them. Do not, and I mean do not push crappy, low-grade products and services down your reader's throats. They hate you and you'll never be able to recover from this loss of reputation. If you intend to make money from affiliate marketing in the long run, stick with high-quality products that will make life easier or offer solid value to your target audience. Your affiliate links should seamlessly be woven into the content. It should feel as if it is a part of the content or topic you are addressing or sharing information about. Don't pitch it as something you are aggressively promoting. Instead, make helpful recommendations to your readers based on your personal experiences.

Rather than simply making your audience the hapless victims of your marketing strategies, guide them. Suggest high-quality products and services that will add value to their lives.

4. Promote your blog or website consistently

Once your affiliate links are built and active, promote your blog or website by going after your target audience. The greater the number of targeted readers you are able to reach out to and draw towards your blog or website, the higher will your income earning potential from referral sales and affiliate marketing commissions.

There are multiple ways to promote your website or blog, including promoting your posts on social media, optimizing your web pages to earn high rankings on search engines and paid advertising mediums (such as Google AdWords and Facebook Ads). Let us keep this for later and focus on the basic steps for now. The first and most important step towards creating any lucrative money-making venture is simply getting started.

Picking the right products on Clickbank

Clickbank is one of the most well-known affiliate networks featuring a large number of digital products across multiple niches. You name the niche, they have it.

Here are some of my best tips for discovering the most profitable products and services on Clickbank:

1. The first pro tip is to avoid promoting too many products or services at a time on your website or blog. Identify a few high-quality, top-selling ones that are relevant to your audience and go with them instead of populating your pages with a million shady offers.

2. As someone looking to make a decent living with affiliate marketing, you need to identify three vital parameters while selecting the right digital information products on Clickbank. If the product's commission happens to be less than 60%, it may not be worthy of your time and efforts. A majority of Clickbank products retail for about $30-70. This means you should garner a minimum of $18/sale. The network has multiple products that offer a higher than 60% payout (some going as much as 70%-75%). Watch out for these products, as these are your most likely winners.

There are a few exceptions to this principle, though. Some expensive products may offer 50 %payout. It is a high priced product, 50% is still a lot of money. Avoid going anywhere below 50 percent, since it is not worth the trouble you'll spend promoting the product.

Yet another exception to this rule is subscription-based products that come with recurring bills, where the affiliate marketer continues to make a commission every time the buyer renews their services. Since recurring commissions are going to make you money each time the subscription is renewed, even a below than 40% commission rate works.

3. The second most important attribute for identifying profitable products on Clickbank is a product's Gravity Rating. This is a ranking given to informational products based on how well they are being sold by other affiliate marketers. If a particular product features a considerably high rating within a given week, it simply means that several marketers are making money from or it is selling like hotcakes. These are currently in-demand products that you can go after.

Again, an exception to this rule is information products that are within the internet marketing or make money online category. What happens is a majority of internet marketers buy a lot of products via their own affiliate link. This helps them get these products at a slashed rate (considering their commission on it). This can tilt the metrics to some extent.

Having said that, you must look out for products with that are valuable, relevant, and promising for your target audience. Low gravity doesn't necessarily translate into low profits. The product may be a new and promising product which hasn't been discovered by many affiliate marketers and has a decent profit potential with little competition. You may help an unknown yet valuable product climb up popularity rankings.

4. How do you evaluate the profitability potential, credibility, and quality of a product? Browse through its sales page. The sales copy of the product or service will reveal a lot about the product's or service's quality. A professionally written and honest sales copy has the potential to covert well. Sales copies that are a mix of logical and emotions do well to entice readers into trying the product or service. Look for products that have sales copies which are surefire winners, as these products or services are most likely to be lapped up by your target audience.

Compare the sales copy of the product you've chosen to promote with other competitor products in the same category. Look at the sales copy of high performing products in the niche. How does the sales copy of the product you've chosen compare with that of the top-selling one? Has your product or service fill a gap left by other products? Does the product have a clear unique selling point? Is the sales copy visually appealing?

Pointers for choosing the Right CPA offers

The reason a lot of internet or affiliate marketing newbies begin with CPA offers is that they can be extremely lucrative. There isn't a need for any purchase on the customer's behalf. All that's required is entering a few details to earn a nice commission in exchange for the information about a potential customer that you've helped the merchant capture.

For example, some merchants or companies may need to capture the customer's name, email, and address to send them some information while others may ask them to fill a form stating their requirements. Each time, a user takes action through your unique affiliate link, you get paid. The most popular CPA offer platforms on the internet are Peerfly and Affiliate.

How do you pick the right affiliate offers? Here's a quick lowdown:

1. Identify CPA offers that can earn you at least $1 per acquisition. Stay miles away from the $0.20 payout offers because unless you get a very large number of users signing up for them, they are just not worth it.

2. The easiest and highest converting offers are zip code offers, where all that is needed on part of the user for you to earn a commission is entering an existing zip code. These offers are high converting and can help you make decent commissions if done right initially. A lot of internet marketers recommend going ahead with health-based CPA offers for beginners as they are known to convert fairly well.

3. Look for CPA programs that provide unrestricted promotion channels. Some affiliate programs come with limitations about where and how they can be promoted, which will restrict your options. For example, programs that can be promoted only via email will work only if you have a considerably exhaustive email list of laser targeted users. As a newcomer, stay away from programs that come with tons of clauses. Ensure you carefully go through the terms and conditions of every program you sign up to avoid courting trouble later.

Create your Website

The first thing to do when it comes to putting together a website is signing up for a hosting service and a domain name (the name following www. for your website or blog). Install WordPress to experiment with the site's look, feel and appearance. Browse through the free themes, which are pre-made layouts. In addition to this, you can also invest in a paid premium WordPress theme to lend it a classier and professional touch.

Populate your website or blog with high quality, rich and relevant content, which provides a definite value to your customers. If there are several websites or blogs operating in your niche, give it a unique angle or stroke to make it unique or highly distinguishable from other blogs in the category. Adopt and develop your own blogging style. For example, there are tons of parenting blogs and you may not stand a fair chance among already existing popular parenting blogs. Opt for a tongue-in-cheek or humorous blog that offers wisdom and insights to parents of teens in a more light-hearted voice. The idea is to stand out or carve a niche for yourself among several similar blogs or websites. This is probably the only way to get noticed and attract a swarm of readers.

Start with at least ten information-rich and in-depth blog posts. If you can't create your own blog posts, hire the services of a professional freelance writer who can make all the difference when it comes to making your content go from humdrum to wow.

Promote your Blog or Website

There are multiple ways to market or promote your blog or website for attracting a large number of focused and interested target readers. Other than following basic search engine optimization tips, the website and blog can be promoted through email, paid advertising channels and social media.

Search Engine Optimization

When internet users actively look for information about a particular topic or niche, they type a series of words and phrases related to what they are looking for to get the required details. The search engine then gets on to the task of tracking the internet for the most relevant and appropriate results based on the users' queries. Thus, an entire list of search results is thrown up based on the words and phrases entered by the user.

To make the task of search engine spiders easier when it comes to locating your pages, include keywords and phrases in your content strategically.

Optimizing your web pages for search engines will help your target readers locate your pages easily, thus helping you build a steady bank of targeted and loyal readers, who are looking for information about your products, services, or niche. As an affiliate marketer, you can cash in on this need to sell them the valuable products and services that fulfill a need. While there are plenty of paid methods for drawing readers to your blog or website, few things beat the power of organic methods like search engine optimization.

Ranking high on a top search engine doesn't happen overnight. It is a slow and complicated process that is often at the mercy of difficult to understand search engine algorithms. Every search engine has its own complex metrics for determining their rankings. Having said that, you cannot discount the contribution of organic searches to the overall success of your blog because this is still where a majority of your targeted and interested customers will originate from. Plus, it's a free traffic source.

Let us look at some search engine optimization tips to boost your blog your website rankings on popular search engines:

- Ensure that every web page's HTML title tag uses a minimum of 2-4 important keywords. They should be no less than 65 characters. Also, avoid filler words such as "and", "to", and others. Use H1, H2 and H3 HTML tags for headers. Do not skip the metatag (which will be the title of your webpage as shown on search engine results) and Meta description (which will be the description of your webpage as shown on search engine results). These may not be seen on your website or blog but they are visible on search engine results.

Meta title and meta description give users a sneak peek of the content on your site or blog, depending on which they decide if they want to visit your site (so it better be awesome). The Meta title should be less than 60 characters, while the Meta description shouldn't exceed 160 characters.

If you have plenty of lists on your blog or site, use the OL or UL tag. Users will be able to scan content on your pages quickly. Use relevant keywords instead of simply stuffing your posts with irrelevant and inappropriate keywords that do not go with the overall theme or niche. Use keywords and key phrases naturally as part of your content.

- Opt for a keyword related domain name without making it look too spam-worthy. Your domain name is your identity; it should be short, catchy, and memorable. Maintain a balance between keeping it brandable and using your most relevant keyword. It should be easy to recall and spell to avoid any confusion. For instance, antiaging ninja, blogging guru, travel authority, etc. are some examples where you are creating a brandable domain name around an important keyword.

- One solid search engine optimization tip is to link articles and blogs within your website to boost on-site optimization. It boosts the stickiness of your website, making users stay on longer on the site or blog as they navigate from one page to another. It is a user-friendly practice that allows readers to access information quickly while enhancing your affiliate site interface.

- Use lots of videos and images to make the site more image and video search ready. At times, people may stumble upon your page while doing a simple Google Images search. To be found in a search engine, don't forget to use alt tags for your pictures with an appropriate keyword that matches your text content.

- It isn't a secret that search engines love in-depth, fresh, and regularly updated content. Add a few other forms of content such as high-resolution videos, Gifs and graphics, and you are set. Keep updating your blog posts on a regular basis by adding content to old blog posts and making edits/changes where required. This ensures that search engine spiders keep frequenting your pages. When you update the content of your site, spiders notice the changes and visit your webpages all over again, thus showing frequently on search result pages.

- Utilize long-tail keywords to bag high rankings on a competitive keyword. Long-tail keywords laser target your audience and help you earn decent rankings even in a fairly crowded keyword. For example, inexpensive cafes may not earn you a high ranking. However, a more detailed keyword such as "inexpensive cafes in

Manhattan" will increase your chances of getting a more targeted user base by showing up on top of search results with minimal competition.

- You are leaving a large chunk of the profit pie for your competitors if you aren't optimizing your site or blog for smartphone users. Over 80% of all internet users carry a smartphone and almost half of the entire web traffic now comes from handheld devices. Go with an optimized WordPress template that is compatible with mobile phones and other handheld devices. Search engines look for multiple factors where the mobile browsing experience is concerned, including browsing speed, download speed, web page usability, web browser compatibility, and much more.

Chapter Four: Blogging Your Way to Riches

A blog is a personal website, online journal or updates authority site where you can share information or your experiences with the world. It can be utilized from everything to writing about your passions to sharing vacation adventures to expressing your thoughts about various issues.

What are the different ways to monetize your blog?

- Promoting or recommending other people's products and services through affiliate marketing.
- Using banner ads and other paid ads.
- Creating and selling your own information products.
- Building your own e-commerce store.
- Displaying advertisement through advertising networks like Google AdSense, where you make money every time a visitor clicks on your advertisement.
- Write paid reviews and information posts for various brands and companies.

- One of the most profitable ways to monetize your blog, which is catching like wildfire nowadays, is to create your own application, software program, and eBooks. If you cannot create them yourself, hire an expert to do it. You just have to create it once and sell it multiple times on your blog for lucrative profits.

How to Build a Blog?

Starting a revenue earning blog is different from just throwing together a bundle of posts, and praying they do well. Let us get down straight to the facts. A Blogging.com study discovered that 81% of bloggers don't even make $100 from their blogs. Now, this speaks more about a blogger's inability to harness the medium effectively than the potential of the medium.

As a passive income earning platform, blogging has plenty of potentials. You just have to learn the ropes and use the medium to its fullest. Running a blog as a source of income involves plenty of things from identifying money making niche to creating awesome blog posts to having a clear monetization plan and exploiting new traffic generation methods.

Steps for Launching a Money-Making Blog

1. Pick a blogging platform

To set up your own blog, you can either go with an independently hosted or self-hosted blog or a free blogging platform. Though you can, of course, begin with a free platform, I wouldn't recommend it if you are serious about blogging as a source of generating income. On the other hand, if you are blogging only for pleasure or to reach out to family and friends through your posts, by all means, go with a free blogging platform.

You won't have the same leverage with free blogging platforms, which often have names such as yourblogname.blogspot.com or yourblogname.tumblr.com. These platforms also come with their own set of policies that you will have to adhere to while using their free services. A majority of free blogging platforms prevent you from displaying advertisements on the blog or utilizing your blog for a commercial objective.

To monetize your blog, go with a self-hosted blogging platform. They give you more control over the contents, layout, and design of the blog. You get a unique domain name unlike a generic one on a free blogging platform. WordPress.org is the best option, to begin with, if you are considering a self-hosted platform. A web hosting plan should set you back by $5-10 a month while a domain should cost you around $10-15/annually.

2. Sign-up for a domain name

To launch a money-making blog, you'll need a unique, memorable, easy to remember, relevant and brandable domain name. An ideal mix is a domain that includes your primary keyword along with a catchy word to make the domain more brandable. The domain name should capture the essence of your website and blog. It should communicate to readers what the blog is all about quickly. You can be the owner of the domain name as long as it is renewed by paying the yearly fee.

Follow the same rules that we looked at while purchasing and selling a domain name. Go with a .com domain name, which is extensively used. Though other domain extensions such as .net, .org or a geographically relevant domain. There are many extensions like .guru, .music or other similar domains for various blog categories. However, .com is still the most popular extension for a website or blog. Avoid hyphens, dashes, dots and other special characters within your domain name.

Although you can skip add-ons offered by domain registrars, you may want to consider Domain Privacy Protection. It protects your private information from going into the public domain. If you don't opt in for Domain Privacy Protection, anybody can view private details such as your contact number, address and other information from a website such as whois.net.

3. Get a hosting account

Pick a steady, dependable, and reliable hosting service that has a consistently good run-up time along with top-notch customer service. A majority of your blog's performance will depend on its speed, download time, and functionality, which is directly affected by your hosting service. While certain bloggers opt to keep their domain name and hosting limited to single service providers, others use different services for their hosting and domain name.

Be very judicious while picking your hosting service, since issues related to downtime, low speed, and unfavorable user experience are almost always related to faulty hosting service. Look out for reviews and in-depth reviews and detailed comparisons of various hosting service providers to go with a time-tested, proven and dependable service.

4. Finalize a blog design and interface

Begin by installing a WordPress blog if you are going with a self-hosted option. You'll receive a confirmation mail from WordPress from your host regarding your account activation. Log-in to the site's control panel. It is a one-click process that doesn't take much time or effort. All you need to do is click "Install WordPress." Once that's taken care of, it will keep loading, and show a notification once WordPress is successfully installed.

Once the installation is completed, the user receives their log in details through email accompanies by your admin URL to log-in with your credentials on the admin panel. The admin panel login URL looks something like this – www.yourblogname.com/wp-admin. Though it may sound a bit intimidating here, it is pretty easy and straightforward when you are actually working with it. Its user-friendly quotient, flexibility, and easy installation process are precisely what makes WordPress one of the most sought after platforms for newbie and seasoned bloggers.

Next, you'll need to select a design template, also referred to as a theme for the blog. The blog's design and layout can be changed by installing new themes at the click of a button. There are tons of customizable, optimized and professional-looking themes that can lend the much needed attractive appearance and user-friendliness to your blog. A site such as Themeforest.net can be used for sourcing premium, paid themes. If you want a more professional and attractive-looking blog, go with a customized theme that is appropriate to your blog's niche.

You can also use plug-ins for your WordPress blogs, which are nothing but software tools that fulfill specific functions related to running the blog. The plug-ins can be used for incorporating contact forms, removing spam, and making the blog search engine optimized. It can also be used for adding images to picture galleries and much more. You now have an up and running a WordPress blog that is self-hosted with a unique domain.

5. Identify a profitable niche

Half your battle is won when you pick a rewarding and profitable niche. Tap into a niche or topic that is not too widely explored but still has decent demand. Narrow it down to make your pages show up in more relevant and focused searches.

Go with a topic that you have a fairly established competency in. For instance, you have studied health and nutrition, and many want to utilize your knowledge for helping readers eat healthily or lose weight. At times new bloggers make the blunder of picking topics where they have competency over topics that simply have a large audience. Let a large audience or popularity not is the only criterion for selecting a niche. Your lack of competency or expertise may eventually make it a losing proposition, especially in the face of completion.

Readers are smart enough to tell knowledgeable bloggers from ones who are simply in it to make big bucks. You will find it hard to keep generating useful, unique and competitive content that isn't found on other similar blogs. Therefore, as a blogger, go with topics you are some expertise in. Without insider knowledge and expertise, you'll keep rehashing content that is already available on the internet and end up annoying your readers. Go with a niche where you have a proven above average competency, which sets you apart from competing blogs. There really is no concept of a best or perfect niche. You just have to identify something you have some knowledge in, and which has a considerable demand.

There are multiple advantages of starting a blog on a topic you feel passionately about. You are less likely to give up out of boredom or de-motivation. Remember, creating a blog is hours of creating content, brainstorming topics, editing the content (you may or may not create the content yourself), uploading blog posts, promoting posts and much more. You will be more driven and stoked about your ideas if you have a deep interest in or passion for the subject. This will invariably result in high rankings for long-tail keywords in search engines. Plus, the lengthier and in-depth content is loved by search engines and also gathers more shares.

Well-written content leads to positive user engagement metrics, which directly affects your search engine rankings. Instead of forever going over multiple niches, begin with a topic/niche you are passionate about, and take action.

Doing Keyword Research using Google Keyword tool

If you want your blog pages to show up on relevant and targeted user searches, you have to use the right keywords (the words and phrases that are most commonly used when your target audience is looking for information, products or services related to your blog topic).

Though the Google Keyword tool fundamentally caters to its AdWords advertisers, bloggers can also gain plenty of information from it. It's like a goldmine of keywords that you can dig into to find plenty of hidden gems.

First, go to the Google Keyword Planner tool. Next, set up your AdWords account, which is required if you plan to use Google's keyword tool. Enter a few details and create a brand new AdWords account. It is a simple process that shouldn't take more than a few minutes.

Then, log in to your AdWords account once its set-up and choose the "Keyword Planner" option under the "Tools" menu.

Now, Keyword Planner will offer three distinct types of tools that can help you dig out keywords related to your niche. You can go with the "search for new keywords using a phrase, website or category" option. Enter your blog niche or category along with a few focused keywords relevant to the blog or niche. Next, choose the "targeting" options.

Also, select the language and country you are planning to target. Again, to make your searches even more accurate and relevant, use filters to discard keywords that don't fulfill the required criteria. For instance, you may not want keywords that have a search volume of less than 3,000 monthly searches.

Once all the required details are entered, select "get ideas" and you'll have access to the keywords. You may or may not be able to get plenty of keyword ideas. However, you will still be able to analyze the search volume of keywords relevant to your niche to determine if it is indeed a profitable niche worth dabbling into.

Once you get the keyword list, copy, and paste it within the search option and get the search volume for it by clicking on "Get search volume." This helps you get an estimation of the number of users who are actively looking for products, services or information related to these keywords.

One pro tip is to avoid over-optimizing your blog at the beginning with too many keywords. It's referred to as keyword stuffing by search engines and doesn't help create a positive impression about your blog in the eyes of these demanding search engines. Focus on high-quality content by incorporating a few keywords initially rather than simply stuffing your posts with keywords for ranking purposes. Remember, humans and not search engine spiders are going to read your content and help it move around. It should be drafted for humans and not search engine bots. Start with 5-7 promising keywords, which have a search volume of more than 1,500/month. There really are no fixed criteria or formula for picking keywords. At times, even a keyword with a measly search volume of 100-200 can prove to be profitable if it has a much-targeted buying audience, who are halfway through the buying cycle or have already made up their mind to buy something and are simply looking around for some offers, deals or comparisons.

A lower search volume doesn't necessarily translate into lower conversions. Similarly, keywords with high search volumes may not necessarily be high converting.

Again, chase long-tail keywords to enjoy higher search engine rankings and a more focused audience, who are truly interested in your products and services. There are several advantages of going with long-tail keywords. You will deal with lower competition, and gather a more focused audience. For example, "remedies for acne marks" may not give you as much leverage as "natural/kitchen remedies for acne marks." Again when it comes to products, exact product names can garner a more focused audience than generic names. For example, "ABC 2 in 1 Rotisserie Grill 2016 model" is more directed than simply "rotisseries."

Writing Blog Posts Readers Love to Share

Setting up your blog and doing keyword research is only half the work done. Now, to run a money-making blog, you have to come up with winning blog topics to keep your readers enthralled. Epic posts are the cornerstone of a busy blog that has lots of readers and a huge following. High readership and audience eventually translate into more money. Well-drafted, slickly presented, and competently researched content earns plenty of social shares and readership. Mediocrity is the single largest reason why most bloggers fail to make money from their blogs. You can set everything else in place but if you don't have awesome content, there's no way your audience is going to return for more. Come up with inspiring, unique and never seen before posts that have unexplored angles and your individual takes about things. Brainstorm ideas to zero down on content people love to share.

Like I mentioned earlier, users on social media love to share content that makes them appear smarter and more well-informed. Keep your blogs enticing, clever and engaging for people to stick on your blog. Not just that, they should also be driven to share it while earning their social currency among their contacts.

I personally love to use apps such as Evernote for noting down ideas for blog posts. Believe me, these ideas can strike you in the unlikeliest of places so always have your app or a pen and paper ready to list them down before they are lost. Inspiration can come in any form. Jot down all your ideas in one place for later reference.

Another super strategy for brainstorming ideas is going to keyowrdtool.io and entering your primary or main keyword. Don't consider the search volume here because we aren't performing keyword research. All we are looking for is blog topic ideas. For example, if you key in "Greece travel guide" there can be multiple keywords associated with the topic such as "Greece travel tips", "Greece travel attractions", "ancient Greek structures to visit", "top Greece bars and nightclubs", "Greece travel scams" and so on. Then there can be "Greece travel guide for solo travelers" or "Greece on a budget for backpackers." Do you get the drift?

Now, this isn't keyword research. You are simply looking for ideas related to your primary topic or keyword. This tip alone can offer you plenty of blog topic ideas. Once you start thinking in the right direction, it isn't tough to come up with close to 100-200 blog topics, in the beginning, depending on your niche. Begin by creating 10-20 blog posts.

Again, a hidden gem that can be wonderfully utilized for uncovering hidden gems in Google's autocomplete feature. You may have noticed that each time you type a couple of words into Google's search bar, it throws up a few suggestions or recommendations based on what it thinks you are looking for. Generate plenty of ideas and suggestions using Google's autocorrect. Each time you enter a keyword, Google will throw up a list of suggestions. For instance, type something like "vacation" and you'll come across a string of suggestions such as "vacation packing tips", "vacation deals for the Caribbean", "vacation travel insurance" and so on. Dig deep into this and there are plenty of topics to explore. Also, there can be a host of viral-worthy blog posts that you can come up with connections to the main topic or keyword. "top 10 must-follow travel blogs", "30 packing hacks no one ever told you about", "20 jobs for location independent nomads" or "40 tips to travel anywhere in the world on a budget."

Why not tap into the power of social media for unearthing hot and trending topics related to your niche. It can be as easy as entering a hashtag such as #vacationnews #travelnews #travel #travelapps #vacations and more on Facebook and Twitter to enjoy exposure to a whole lot of potentially winning topics. You'll most likely you currently trending and popular topics related to your niche, which can be converted into share-worthy blog posts. Look at visuals, tweets and people's posts for inspiration.

Even a tweet as simple as, "I want to meet new folks from different cultures while traveling across the world" can inspire a blog post such as "valuable tips for making friends on your travels" or "how to approach strangers or finding a hot date on your travels" or "myths about solo travel busted." Again, you get the idea right? There is inspiration all around you. Simply look for places that others wouldn't consider and you'll come across a minefield of blog topics.

I also find niche magazines, journals, and publications to be hot sources for blog topic ideas. They have plenty of engaging topics to wow readers that you can take inspiration from. Ideally, find topics that offer your readers information that isn't too common or lend a common topic a unique angle while presenting it. For example, there are hundreds of blog posts about "top 20 bars in New York City." You will increase the chances of your post being read and shared if you come up with something such as, "Did you know about these secret underground bars in New York City?"

A lot of popular bloggers use Hubspot's Topic Generator tool for finding killer blog topic ideas. Simply enter a few nouns related to the niche or topic and the tool will display tons of suggestions and recommendations. If you are looking for topics that are currently enjoying a huge run of popularity on social media, go to BuzzSumo. Enter your topic and the site will throw up a list of the blog posts (related to your topic) that have gathered maximum social shares recently. This can give you a fair amount of idea on the kind of posts that are performing well virally within your niche.

Another goldmine of topic ideas that few bloggers and internet marketers consider is content aggregation sites such as Quora, Yahoo Answers and Reddit. People are actively seeking answers to their queries, challenges, and problems here, which mean you, can come across plenty of winning blog post topics here. People asking questions means they are actively seeking information or solutions.

Fill this need, and you'll wow your target audience. For example, someone may post a question about the "best applications for people seeking guidance on investing their money." Ta-da! This can give you an idea to write an in-depth blog post about the best investment-related applications.

You have a ready to create blog posts such as "top 20 useful apps for investment newbies" Everything is available at your fingertips really, all you need to do is be a little resourceful and dig around for fresh and inspiring ideas. Keep finding interesting, engaging and fresh blog topics to keep your blog regularly updated.

Proven Traffic Generation Tips for Bloggers

Of course, you don't want to create a pretty-looking and high-quality content blog only to watch it turn into a ghost land that has no visitors. Your chance of earning long-term passive income from the blog is directly proportionate to the number of visitors visiting your blog and, subsequently, the conversion rate. It a game of numbers at the end of the day! The higher the number of people you manage to attract to your blog, the higher will be your conversions and subsequently the revenue you earn from the blog.

Here are my winning tips for attracting a swarm of visitors to your website or blog:

1. I've mentioned a few tips in the earlier chapter for search engine optimizing your blog posts and pages. Incorporate your primary keyword within the blog title. Use the important h1, h2, and h3 tags. Then, link to internal blog posts, and don't forget to utilize alt text for your images. Meta titles and descriptions are always a good SEO practice. Avoid keyword stuffing. Keep in mind all these pointers. There are many more aspects to search engine optimization (which is a very fast topic) but these are good pointers to get you started.

WordPress has a plug-in called Yoast, which will inform you about how optimized your blog posts are, and the changes you can make to make these posts more search engine friendly. Take care of Search Engine Optimization and you'll increase your chances of attracting plenty of focused and relevant organic traffic.

2. Have you heard about guest blogging? It is one of the best ways to gain exposure and traction not just among your followers but also other blog readers and followers. Guest blogging is nothing but creating exceptionally valuable and high-quality posts for other popular blogs and websites to increase your reach and built the reputation of an expert within the field.

Outreach is a becoming a much sought after way for networking with other bloggers and influencers to increase your own audience base. Approach popular bloggers for guest blogging opportunities. Ensure though that blog posts you create for these popular blogs as a guest blogger are high-quality, well-researched, detailed, and offer readers a valuable take away. You need to create an authoritative and credible reputation for yourself within your industry or niche. Guest blog posts can help you pitch yourself as an expert in the domain. In the author bio of your guest post, you can include information about yourself along with a link to your blog.

Invite other known names within your niche to write guest posts for your blog to increase yours as well their blog readership. Once known bloggers within the industry create guest posts for your blog, they are most likely to share it on social media accounts. I mean who doesn't want to present themselves as experts among their followers? Once a link to a post on your blog is shared on the social media of a well-known blogger, you can gain plenty of page views and shares from their followers. This helps increase your blog traffic and social shares.

A lot of people inquire about approaching influencers and authorities within a domain. It can be as simple as finding that the top influencers in a genre are with the help of simple searches on Twitter, Instagram, and Facebook. Simply type your topic name or primary keyword, followed by "influencer" to come up with a list of key influencers and authorizes within your industry.

Next, approach these influencers by drafting a well-written and professional mail about associating with them for your promising and upcoming blog. Be specific while complimenting them but don't make it seem like flattery. Ideally, mention a couple of their posts that you enjoyed reading and why. This can tell them you've been diligently following them and they may relent.

There are several blogging communities such as ProBlogger where you can network with influencers within your niche and even cross-promote each other's blog posts for a wider audience. If you want to attract the attention of a blogger or influencer within your industry, leave informative, factual, and insightful comments on their blog posts. They will more often than not take note of it, and it'll be easier to approach them as an active follower/reader of their blog.

If you are mentioning an influencer within your blog post, don't miss mentioning or tagging them in a Facebook post or Tweet while promoting the post. This way your post will be displayed on their feed, thus giving you the much-needed exposure.

3. Industry round-ups. Drafting industry-based round-ups are one of the most popular ways to gain plenty of exposure from the followers of not just one but several popular bloggers. This is a win-win situation for everyone involved. The way it works is you get several experts in your domain to feature in a valuable round-up where you pose them a question or

ask them to share their tips, suggestions, or views about something that your viewers want to know.

For instance, if you are a beauty or blogger, you may want to ask experts or influencers in the domain their number one tip for keeping their skin looking young and glowing. Then again, if your blog is about making money online, you may want to ask influencers and popular web marketers their number one traffic generation tip. Everyone wants to be seen as an expert in their domain by offering valuable information.

Again, there are high chances of these experts sharing this round-up) in which they feature) on their social media accounts. This can give you plenty of exposure among the followers of not just one but several influencers. Can you imagine your reach? Come up with a list of questions that your target audience is actively seeking answers or solutions for, and fill that gap by posing the questions to these experts.

4. Use the power of content aggregator sites. Post your blog page links on aggregator sites. Ensure that you don't answer questions in a shoddy manner just to leave behind a spammy link. Leave your blog link

behind only when you've helped the user with some useful, relevant, and high-quality information. Post your links only if you think the blog post will help the user get what he/she is looking for or will add some value to what they are seeking. Content aggregator sites have the potential to offer you plenty of focused and directed traffic if used well. Just avoid spamming it with your blog links and you'll do fine. Also, ensure your answers are well-researched, unique, detailed, and offer the user an actionable takeaway. Stay away from stating the obvious or filling it with fluff just to push in a link.

5. Create a loyal community and following. Making money from blogging isn't simply about putting together a few posts and pushing people to your blog posts. You need to create a loyal following and close-knit community feeling among readers to make them keep coming back for more. Create a place where your audience can interact with each other, share their thoughts about specific blog topics and feel a strong sense of community. Give them a more conversational, engaging, communicative, and interactive platform.

While commenting on blog posts is fine, building a group or community around something that is common among your readers or brings them together is a good idea. Get these users to be more interactive by building a Facebook group. Your audience can post their problems; seek suggestions, share experiences, and more related to the niche. For example, let's say your niche is about parenting, you can create groups for new mothers or single parents where your audience can discuss challenges and tips related to better parenting practices. Ensure that you create rules to maintain the community's standards and decorum.

6. Get active on social media. Creating awesome content and hoping that your audience will somehow find you are equivalent to staying at home without an internet connection and praying that your soul mate will somehow find you. It doesn't work this way. You have to place your content where your target audience is likely to find it. Be more proactive when it comes to driving a swarm of readers to your blog by utilizing resourceful and creating traffic generation techniques. Use multiple techniques and test one that works well for you by analyzing the results of your traffic from different sources. Then, scale up the techniques that work.

Gauge which social media channel can give you the best traction-based on the nature of your niche and content format. For example, Twitter can be wonderful for including catchy and snappy quotes from your blog post along with a link to the blog. Platforms such as Pinterest and Instagram can work well for more graphically inclined niches. Facebook is good for long and detailed blog posts that have the potential to go viral through several shares.

One tip that I'd like to share here if you really want social media users to take the trouble of checking out your blog posts and master the art of creating attention-grabbing and impossible to ignore headlines. Look at headlines of viral sites such as ViralNova and Buzzfeed. It is virtually impossible to ignore them and move on without clicking on the links. You must be able to trigger your reader's interest and curiosity through the headlines. However, also bear in mind that the content matches your lofty headlines. Don't deliver a turkey after promising a high-quality post.

Some internet marketers discover that posting a certain amount of blog posts each week increase their traffic by a considerable percentage. Figure out your ideal number of posts and stick to it once you discover the number of weekly posts that give you maximum traction. When you decide to scale it up, increase the number of blog posts.

7. Did you know that YouTube sends the highest number of focused and engaged social media audience among the entire social media lot? If you aren't using the power of YouTube, you may lose a lot of money. Record high-quality, engaging, relevant, entertaining, and informative videos for driving traffic to your website or blog.

8. If you want to advertise your website or blog on a popular blog, instead of paying them hefty advertising fees, participate in banner exchange. There may be blogs that complement your blog, where both you and the other blogger can benefit from a banner exchange without spending money. For example, lets you have a travel blog, you can swap banner ads with travel insurance or digital cam blog.

9. Do not overlook the power of building your own list. Your list is your wealth. When you rely on Google or Facebook for a major chunk of your traffic or source of income, you are at the mercy of their constantly fluctuating policies and regulations. With one update or change in policy, you can lose your source of income

overnight. This isn't to scare you. However, your email list is something that you have complete control over.

Using details of your target audience, you can keep sending links to new posts, newsletters, sales offers, and much more. This can generate plenty of repeat views and purchases, and ultimately a loyal following. Use opt-in software that lets visitors subscribe to your newsletters or future updates/communication. One good tip for increasing your opt-ins is giving away freebies such as an information-packed eBook that they wouldn't find elsewhere, a short report, a handy checklist or a course.

This serves a two-way purpose. It establishes you as an authority in your domain while also giving you access to their details for future communication. Then again, you can include a Call to Action within your Facebook page to get your readers/followers to take action. Use an application such as Rafflecopter for creating sweepstakes, contests, and giveaways those readers can participate in after filling in details like their name and email address.

Chapter Five: Drop shipping on Amazon FBA

Drop shipping is one of the easiest and most profitable ways to generate passive income online. Owing to its low start-up costs, flexibility and easy set-up, plenty of budding entrepreneurs prefer this business model. To begin with, you don't require physical space for storing your products. Then, you don't need to maintain an inventory of products waiting to be sold. Of course, Amazon FBA (Fulfillment by Amazon) needs an upfront investment. However, if you are going for other drop shipping services, there may be no upfront investment involved. All you need to do is get orders from customers, forward these orders to your drop shipping company, and let them take care of the rest (including shipping, delivery, transaction handling and more). Both you and the drop shipping company earn profits from the sale. You source your products at a lower price from the drop shipping company and determine the price you want to sell it at, thus having complete control over your profit.

There are several advantages of signing up for the Amazon FBA plan though since the reach and exposure offered by the retailer is incomparable with most platforms. The beauty of Amazon's FBA business model is that you do get started from just about anywhere without having to maintain a product inventory. Amazon will do everything from storing your products in their warehouse to delivering it to customers. What's more? They will also handle customer service for you.

Though Amazon FBA is a simple, flexible and convenient way to get started, it is by no means a get rich quick business model. You'll need to spend a lot of time researching popular product categories to identify products that sell well. Then, there is the task of finding cost-effective suppliers and fixing buying costs.

Once the system is in place though, it can be a completely automated process where you don't have to do much other than probably promote your products. Everything is handled by Amazon.

Tried and Tested Strategies for Identifying Popular Products

To start with, look for massive bargains and deals on products available locally in your neighborhood or city. Measure these up against products already listed on Amazon. Do your products have the potential to outperform competing products in terms of price, quality, uniqueness or any other factor? Check out if similar products are selling well. A good reference point is the Amazon Bestsellers compilation. At what price can you sell the product? As a thumb rule, a product rank lower than 1,000 is a broader category means the product is doing fairly well and can be considered for sales.

One smart strategy is to register for newsletters from wholesalers or be on the mailing list of stores such as Ikea. You'll receive tons of special offers, discounts, and promos simply by going through their site. If there is a discount available for a limited period on items that have reasonable demand, purchase them in bulk to keep it in your inventory. You can sell the products for pretty profits later. Ensure you factor in Amazon's fees while determining the final selling price of the product.

Private label products are also popular with sellers on Amazon FBA. Basically, you find manufacturers or wholesale suppliers from whom you can source high quality and in-demand products in bulk. These products are then sold under your private brand name or label. You position yourself as the manufacturer of the product without going through the process of creating it on your own.

The Required Investment for Amazon FBA

You need to invest some money for building a product inventory on Amazon FBA, unlike traditional drop shipping. Other than the cost of purchasing your products, you may need to foot the forwarding charges. Then there may be a referral fee, some subscription charges, and inventory storage charges. Enter all the fees and expenses you are likely to incur in the FBA calculator for it to suggest the ideal selling price.

Begin small if you aren't sure of the demand and response to your products just to test the buyer market. If you are simply trying the FBA business model or planning to sell high priced products in smaller numbers, you can opt for the $0.99 fee per transaction subscription option. This option can be used for a maximum of 40 products each month. However, if you plan to sell low priced products in large volumes to earn a profit, then it may make sense to opt for the $39.99 monthly charge. The monthly subscription fee also gives to access to business reports.

Chapter Six: Building Passive Income with Udemy Courses

This is another super passive income business model where you create a product once and keep earning on it several times. Setting up channels for raking in recurring income is the secret for building passive income in the long haul. Udemy is one of the most reliable and popular platforms for people looking to earn from their skills. There are courses on everything from how to read tarot cards to playing the guitar to being a life coach. If you are an established blogger or authority in your domain, these courses can also be sold through your own blogs or social media pages. However, for beginners, who haven't yet built a steady stream of loyal followers, Udemy is probably a good place to begin.

1. Choose a topic

It's a no brainer that you must have fair knowledge or expertise in something if you wish to earn from creating a course around it. Use all your educational qualifications, certifications, talents, and experiences to pitch yourself as an expert in the field. All of us have mastery over some topics or skills. It can be anything from Italian cooking to floral decorations. Just pick a topic you are passionate about or have established expertise in, and you're good to go. For example, let us say you studied a subject like sociology at the university level. You can create topics around social relationships or interpersonal relationships such as "Networking with people is social gatherings for business" or "being the ultimate dating ninja." Keep the topic relevant to your area of expertise, education, and experience, which will offer you an edge over others.

Research is critical to the process of putting together a course. If you can't do extensive research yourself, hire someone to take it upon your behalf. Remember the course should offer learners high-value not crappy, rehashed information that can be sourced from the internet. If you expect people to pay to learn something, it better offers them a unique value proposition that can't be found elsewhere. Make your course comprehensive, in-depth and, one of a kind.

2. Make the course

Udemy is easy to use and the straightforward platform even if you don't have any prior experience selling virtual courses. Register as an instructor on Udemy by following their instructions. Begin by creating an outline of what exactly you plan to teach before uploading your course or training videos. It helps to title or tag each section (don't number it) and then shuffle around their order logically once you complete creating all videos. Trainers often end up moving around the sequence with an easy drag-drop option so it is best not to number them.

One mistake that plenty of course creators make is recapping the same modules or including filler content, which makes them ineffective. Also, avoid spending a lot of time introducing various modules. Most people watch all the videos within a day or two, which means they don't need too much recapping and are able to pick bits and pieces of details that are important for them.

3. Record your videos

You need a quiet and distraction-free place to record a video, preferably with a white wall background. Use a high-quality webcam for the purpose of recording your Udemy course video. Both Logitech, as well as Blue Yeti, feature clear visuals and sound. You'll have to educate yourself about the finer aspects of recording and editing videos. There are applications such as Movie Maker, which can be used for making your own effective course videos.

4. Market the course like a pro

Pretty similar to other virtual income techniques, this can be as simple or challenging as you want it to be. The thing about Udemy is, it promotes courses that are already faring well or ranking at the top within various sections. This is a bit of a never circle, which means your course won't really be featured among the top-ranked or aggressively promoted courses if it isn't marketed well by you, to begin with.

This simply means you will have to take on the early promotional and marketing efforts yourself to garner a minimum of 50-100 registrations for the course while also bagging some reviews to give your promotional efforts a decent kickstart. These courses can be set up on couponing websites or specialized forums.

Distribute the course for free among your social circle or launch it at an early bird, discounted price. Create a helpful noise around it and make it more reachable to people at discounted prices in the beginning when you don't really have any sales or reviews to validate its quality. Urge social contacts and family members to leave behind favorable reviews.

If you can, create a YouTube channel for marketing the course. Include an engaging and compelling promotional video for your course. Don't forget to include a link at the end of the video. Keep it short, arresting, and informative. Let it whet the appetite of your target audience without satisfying their hunger. What can you include in this video? Everything from primary course objectives to what students can take back from the course to reviews and testimonials from students.

At times, people ask me why anybody would be willing to pay for information that is available on the internet with a little research. This is true for eBooks, courses, and other informational products. The thing is, sometimes people just don't have the time, inclination, or energy to browse through tons of erratically laid down information from multiple sources. If you are able to offer them everything they need to know in an easy to read/follow format in a clear and visually pleasing manner, they will be more than willing to pay for it. Time is money and anything that helps people save time is worth it from their perspective.

Create guides that solve people's problems or fill a clear need and they will be more than happy to pay for it. Research and create the content in an easily digest-able format to save your users' time and efforts. Everything should be readily available at their fingertips. Once people are convinced that all the information they are seeking is easily available in an easy to comprehend and access format, they'll be sold.

Use tools such as Google Keyword Planner to research the most appropriate and popular keywords for the course to ensure that the course landing page is optimized for searches. People who are actively looking to learn skills or information related to what you are offering should be able to locate it easily. Pick keywords that can be easily converted and may not have much competition (but are still fairly popular) over high-search ones.

Let us look at an example to understand this. Something like weight loss exercises can have an extremely high volume of searches since there are many people looking to lose weight. However, when you say something such as "cardio exercises for weight loss" or "5-minute weight loss exercises for those pressed for time", your chances of conversion are automatically higher because you are targeting a narrower user base that is already looking for very targeted and specific information. They may be halfway past the buying cycle already. These people may have already made up their minds about signing up for a specific course and may need a little convincing to take action in your favor. They may be looking around for reviews or course contents. Using action-oriented keywords is a sensible strategy because it helps expose your page to people who are already halfway through the action taking cycle.

Once you witness a steady stream of traffic, Udemy follows suit and begins promoting the course. This helps boost your organic traffic building effort. This traffic can increase your profit potential considerably without much effort on your part. Thus, it helps to market the course aggressively on your own in the beginning to grab Udemy's attention and gain its much-needed leverage for late marketing and promotional efforts.

Again it's a game of numbers. The more courses you have listed on Udemy, the higher are your chances of converting it into a rewarding and profitable income source.

5. Build a complete and long term income plan

This may not be the best place to begin if you are looking to build a full time online passive income business. However, it is a good secondary source of income until you become an established course creator with several million followers and students who swear by your courses. As far as possible, have control over or try to gain ownership over your enterprises overselling on third-party platforms. Of course, when you are a newbie looking to sink your teeth into the big bad world of online money making, you will need these platforms for their popularity and huge user base. However, at the end of the day, you will be subject to their policies, regulations, and sudden changes. Retain as much control over your profits and business a possible by selling on your own platform.

Udemy can also get you plenty of earlier customers while making you a known name within your field. Once you build an established reputation, consider creating courses on your own websites along with unique membership programs and subscriptions (where you can earn recurring income each time the user renews their subscription). There are plenty of content formats for training including podcasts and Facebook live (which is available even after you're done training live).

One pro tip for making your courses popular on Udemy is to create and publish free courses on Udemy while promoting your products/services in the bonus section as per the platform's guidelines. Users can also build their own blogs or websites and create compelling teasers of their Udemy courses to guide interested visitors to the Udemy website for purchasing the entire course. If you want them to head back to your website or blog, use the bonus section. Then again, some course creators have their courses published on their blog/website and Udemy (which becomes like a secondary income source). There is a lot of money to be made in imparting online training. You need to be creative and resourceful enough to tap into it.

Chapter Seven: Get Rich Flipping Domains

Owning domains on the internet is like owning a piece of real estate. Think of them as virtual properties that can be bought at a particular price and later sold at a higher price to reap rich profits. If done correctly, domain flipping can make you plenty of passive income. Here's a detailed guide to making money flipping internet domains.

You've probably never used Fb.com to log in to the social networking site of Facebook. However, that didn't stop Facebook from purchasing the domain for a princely $8.5 million just so no one can ever use it. Now, I know a majority of domains are not worth that amount and this is just the extreme end of the spectrum. The point here is that domain buying and selling can be an insanely profitable business that can help you earn unimaginably high profits without doing much. Look at business and domain flipping sites and you'll find promising domains selling at ridiculous prices. Some people make a comfortable living solely by flipping domains. To be a master in the game, you need to quickly pick up promising domains (I'll let you in on what makes a domain promising later in the chapter) and where it can be sold for a decent profit.

Identifying and Scouting for Valuable Domains

A decent domain name is one that has the potential to help a business grow. If you consider some of the highest selling domain, you'll find a few common attributes. In a majority of cases, the domains are short, unique, memorable, brandable, relevant, and easy to remember and limited to a single word. Single-word domains are generally ideal as they have a high recall value, and are simpler to type. People find it easier to share type and memorize single word domains.

Preferably, go with a .com option. Though there is multiple extension choices nowadays, .coms still remain the most popular extensions because whenever people think about accessing a site on the internet, by default they think of it as XYZ (site name).com. Where the profitability of domain flipping is concerned, .com is almost always preferred over other extensions. It is simply a matter of cognitive fluency. Whether you think it's boring or not, .com extensions still remain the most widely recognized and known of all extensions. If.com is not available for a specific domain name; try to lay your hands on a .co or .net domain. You can also use geographically relevant domain extensions such as .co.uk for the United Kingdom or .ca for Canada. This holds value for businesses that are local to those countries, which means you may end up limiting your market unless you are sure business in the United Kingdom or Canada will be prepared to pay a premium for these domain names or it has high value for a local business.

Keep in mind that a domain name is useful for businesses only if it helps them bag new customers, readers, or viewers. It should help them attract new members of their target audience. Premium domains are generally exact or near-exact matches of common terms used by people while searching for related information on popular search engines. How does one assess the search volume to identify popular domains? Use Google's, Keyword Tool.

Another important criterion that holds a lot of weight when it comes to determining the value of a domain name is its age. Search engines look for a domain's age as one of their ranking criteria. The more aged or older the domain name, the more valuable it is believed to be. Domain names can be found on domain registrar sites such as GoDaddy and NameCheap.

Remember to stay away from domains that have hyphens or numbers in them, which take away from their brand-able quotient. Such domains barely have any recall value or memorable appeal. For instance, there is a huge difference between freshvegetables.com and fresh-vegetables.com or freshvegtables054.com.

Also, you would think that spoofing a popular brand or celebrity domain name can be highly profitable. For example, say a variation of Cola-Cola. However, this can qualify as an infringement of copyright, which can lead to a massive legal battle. If you have even the slightest doubt about certain domains, talk to a legal professional before going ahead to prevent future hassles. Also, some domains may have been penalized by Google earlier, which significantly lowers the value of a domain.

Selling Domains

After purchasing a high-value domain name, you may want to sell it for a high profit to people who would gain real value from it. There are multiple websites that let you list domains in exchange for a percentage from the sale. These are arbitrage sites such as Flippa. Flippa is one of the most popular and established platforms for buying and selling domains. It is a widely recognized marketplace, where domain sales are often known to go up to six figures.

Keep realistic expectations when it comes to selling your domains based on their worth and value for the potential buyer. Every domain name (however promising it appears to you) doesn't sell for millions. Each domain has its own potential. Even if you don't sell domains often, even one sale worth thousands can help you make a decent living.

Keep patience, which is an important virtue when it comes to being a domain flipping master. Don't simply sell a domain at any price higher than what you've purchased it for. Know the true worth of your domain, and learn to speculate if you can get more value by waiting and selling it later. Don't simply purchase domains randomly because you believe you can sell them. There are plenty of factors involved in each sale. Success doesn't come overnight. You will come across both – domains that will never sell or ones that are winners which don't need much effort to sell. Bear in mind you'll take a while to master the game.

Chapter Eight: Slaying the Passive Income Game with Real Estate

Now, if you have enough money to invest in real estate, there are plenty of ways to make that money work for you. There are multiple ways to make passive income from the real estate including earning rentals on your property and flipping homes.

Flipping homes can be highly lucrative and profitable but it isn't easy. One needs to understand the dynamics of the real estate market as well as changing trends to make the most of it. Much like flipping domains, you need to understand what the property selling worth it after it is renovated or spruced up. It involves some amount of speculation, research, and understanding of the number game.

Here's a step by step real estate flipping guide:

1. Put your money in the right neighborhood

You must have in-depth knowledge about the market in various neighborhoods before zeroing down on one that looks ideal from the investment perspective and has plenty of potentials. You may fix the house and make it stunning; however, you can't do much about its neighborhood. So don't just look at homes that can be transformed. Also, look for neighborhoods when it comes to evaluating and selecting a property.

Some things to consider are, how much are homes typically selling for in the neighborhood? Also, what are the types of houses that are rare within the neighborhood? For example, in a neighborhood filled with three-bedroom ranches, a four-bedroom Victorian home may be much sought after, and therefore command a premium price. You can browse through websites such as Redfin and Zillow for information about the latest sales.

Research market trends that are likely to influence home prices in the future. You may need to do in-depth research to determine speculative figures for the price of the property next year or after the next couple of years. For example, let's say a new hotel is coming up in the neighborhood, which is slated to go on a massive hiring drive. This could suggest that rental prices may well increase. This will translate into higher rentals among the multi-family homes too. Know market trends in and around the neighborhood you plan to put your money in.

While doing your research, you may come across markets promising markets with an inventory that is under six months. However, this isn't an indication of factors such as shadow inventory, which can be present in a specific neighborhood. The neighborhood may have a high concentration of foreclosed homes (which in turn can bring down prices).

Another factor that can pose an issue when it comes to renovating or selling the home can be a crime. You may have a tough time finding potential buyers in a crime-infested neighborhood. Go with nicer and more pleasant neighborhoods, though it may be challenging to find winsome deals here. In the long run, it helps to save plenty of stress, heartbreak, and frustration.

2. Identifying the right property

Once you've zeroed down on the right neighborhood, the next step involves identifying the right property to fix and flip. Go through referrals, the MLS, and local classified advertisements to identify the perfect fix and flip deals.

I personally like identifying flip-worthy properties by walking or driving through the neighborhood to keep an eye out for vacation houses. At times, the owners may be lagging on their mortgage payments or ready to move out. This way you can identify several fix and flip houses that can fetch you a decent profit.

Another value tip is to network with brokers, contractors, and other real estate related connections to get referrals on unoccupied homes that are up for sale. The thing is, real estate brokers and professionals, do not always have the time or connections to flip houses profitably. They may refer it to someone with a good reputation for a small finder's fee.

Use the MLS or multiple listing service platforms to the fullest. The objective is to watch out for properties that ate wrongly listed, in deteriorating condition, or feature a smaller number of bedrooms in comparison to its square footage. For instance, a 3,500 square foot home with 2 bedrooms can easily be transformed into a 3 bedroom home. This can help you sell it at a much higher price.

Direct mail or sending yellow letters are good ways to communicate with homeowners who may show a willingness to sell their home at a reduced rate. These letters are often left at the door of distressed looking houses. It is generally a more personal and handwritten note that conveys to the buyers that you are keen on purchasing the home. House owners about to face foreclosure are often desperate to sell their homes fast. Being prompt is the key as these are people looking for the best price to get rid of homes that are proving to be a liability for them.

3. Working out the potential after renovation value

This is where your math comes into play. Before buying a house for flipping purposes, you must determine its ARV or after repair value. The best way to do is by checking out how many similar homes in the neighborhood and has recently sold for. What renovations are you planning to undertake, and much have a home with similar renovations and area sold for recently in the neighborhood?

Remember your objective is not just to sell the home at a price that is higher than the price you purchased it for but also higher than the purchase price and renovation expenses. Then there are plenty of other fees and costs involved such as the contractor fees. Use the 70% rule as a smart flipper. Try and keep your expenses within 70 %of the house's anticipated After Repair Value. Anything more than this and the deal may just not be worth the effort.

Then there will be holding expenses. Say, the house takes 6-8 months to sell from the time of purchase. This means you'll also have to take care of expenses related to owning the property, which can add up expenses. All these costs need to be factored in when it comes to determining the final selling price of the home if you want to make a decent profit.

4. Avoid scrounging on the home inspection

Once you've zeroed in on a home you which have considerable renovation potential, you'll need professional home inspection services. Though you can do the home inspection yourself, it is highly recommended that you hire a licensed inspector to check for any major repairs and renovations. Spending some hundreds on a professional home inspector can help you save the deal, which makes it more than worth the investment.

Some of the most common deal killers are large foundation cracks, damaged chimneys, worn-out electric wiring, and environmentally hazardous oil tanks.

5. Financing project

How are you going to finance the home and its fixing project? A majority of traditional lenders do not show keenness to invest in poor condition houses, which makes it challenging for beginners to fund these buy and fix projects. It gets worse if you have a low net worth or an unsteady source of independent income. There are a few other options to consider in such a scenario.

Home flipping newbies or those with a low credit score can borrow from hard money lenders. These are groups of money lenders that lend for the purpose of house flipping. They are hugely popular among home flippers because money lenders' often focus on a property's after renovation value rather than the credit score, income or experience of the flipper. Then again, you can also get a private money lender to fund your project. To pick the most reputed lenders, talk to seasoned home flippers or look for contact details on a reputed national directory.

You can also opt for a regular bank loan or get a real estate crowdfunding project to fund your fix and flip project. Crowdfunding typically involves a big investor pool where you can get access to money immediately. While money lenders and hard lenders can release money within a couple of weeks, crowdfunding releases the money to you for only a couple of days.

6. Assembling the team

You will be closely working with a lot of people including multiple contractors, inspectors, legal professionals, appraisers and more during your fix and flip projects. It helps to build a strong network of relationships with these people if you plan to make house flipping a reliable source of long-term income. Though you may need more than one contractor, find one who is reliable, affordable and delivers work in a timely manner.

This means you won't have to change your contractor each time you take on a fix and flip project. Find someone trustworthy, budget conscious and focused on turning out high-quality jobs. Apart from a general contractor, you may need several other contractors such as a plumber, electrician and so on. If it is your first flip project, you can get referrals from existing flippers. Alternately, you can also ask for referrals from existing contractors. For instance, you can ask the plumber to refer an electrician since these contractors tend to work on many projects together and have a good network.

It is a good practice to get the contractor to update you at least once or twice a week. You should also closely monitor the job on a regular basis to ensure work is going as per the stipulated schedule. There is absolutely no substitute for those Home Depot runs where you need to check everything in person. You'll know exactly how something looks in person, and may also end up grabbing some winning deals. If you are a flipping newbie, I'd highly recommend sourcing materials by checking them out in person rather than purchasing them online.

However, if you are confident and are on the same page as the contractor about what materials to use, use this time and effort to identify your next deal.

While some flippers pay their contractors on a weekly basis, it is highly recommended that you pay them according to milestones accomplished. It can be something like a starter deposit, then the next payment once the floors are set in, followed by a complement of the kitchen. If you opt for a hard loan, the lender will generally release funds based on the submitted contractor service invoices.

Some of the most popular renovation jobs are redoing floors. This can impact a home's price and demand considerably. Then there are tile jobs in the bathroom and kitchen. Take on budget beautification and fixing tasks such as adding mirrors, replacing cabinets, adding gorgeous looking bath fixtures and changing kitchen appliances. Even small changes like these can go a long way when it comes to increasing your return on investment. If it's your first flip project, avoid taking on big renovations unless you are sure it will help you gain lucrative returns. These renovation jobs are cost-effective, relatively easier, and can enhance the overall appearance of the home. Adding a room is another popular fix job when it comes to flip and fix projects. Though it can be an expensive and time-consuming affair (you may also have to obtain the required permits), the job may end up offering you a lucrative return on investment.

A majority of home buyers nowadays prefer open plans. If there are closed rooms, you can take up an opening enclosed spaces project to increase the home's sale value. Basements can be converted into living spaces. Though legally certain cities may not permit the basement to be termed a bedroom, homebuyers can still use the additional space for a home office, entertainment den, or guest room.

7. Selling the home

There is considerable debate about whether non-realtors should sell the house themselves or hire the services of a professional realtor. There are plenty of advantages of hiring a professional realtor, though the downside is it is going to eat into your profit. In exchange for their fees, realtors will aggressively market the home within their network of buyers and realtors on MLS.

You may get access to a larger buyer base and even bag a lucrative selling price compared to if you go about selling the home on your own. So, the realtor fees may well be more than worth it. However, if you are confident about making the sale yourself, go ahead with it after exercising due caution and ensuring everything is in place, especially if its own first flipping project.

Step-by-Step process for Rental Property Investment

1. Keep a plan ready

There are several different kinds of rental properties that are available in the real estate market – single-family houses, multi-family homes, commercial properties, vacation rental properties, and so on. Narrow down your options based on market trends, buyer preferences, and other factors determining the value of properties in the neighborhood of your choice. Of course, you don't always have to stick to a single property type but it helps to narrow it down and concentrate on one type in the beginning. Read books about rental investment, listen to informative podcasts, and gather insider tips from other rental investors.

2. Choose your market

One doesn't need to invest in their neighborhood but it helps when you are starting out. Depending on your plan, financial objectives and market trends, you may also want to invest in a property far away from your place of residence. For example, if you live in the downtown region, it may not make sense to invest heavily in a downtown home if you don't have the requisite investment funds. In such a scenario, a home in a family-oriented and upcoming suburb may be your best bet.

Define your market. What type of renters are you targeting? Which are the areas people enjoy living in? Where are rental property prices likely to increase? Which areas are having low crime rates? Which properties are hot among tourists and vacationers?

Talk to realtors, local residents, and business owners and property managers and investors to get a good idea of the property market in the area you've zeroed down on.

3. Put together an effective team

To be a successful rental investor, you need to build a team of professionals that can be relied upon for assistance in the future. As an investor, you will need a real estate agent (to help you identify deals and determine market trends), a moneylender (to finance your property purchases), a property manager (to guide you about existing rental prices and neighborhoods, and a contractor (to take care of repairs and renovations). You can also network with other investors or reach out and build relationships with on sites such as biggerpockets.com. It helps you ask for referrals and recommendations before putting together your handy squad.

4. Financing deals

There are multiple ways to get your deals financed. Some of them are conventional loans, private loans, partnership deals, commercial property loans and more. Zero down on an option that best fits your financial goals and business strategy.

5. Start getting leads

Start getting leads now from your realty agent, referrals, and direct mails. You may also consider the driving around option. Get the leads flowing if you want to crack winsome rental investment deals.

6. Scrutinize deals

However much you hate math, you'll have to play around with numbers to negotiate winning real estate deals. Analyze property deals to make these numbers work in your favor. Keep in mind your financial goals while doing math. For instance, let us say your goal is to have a cash flow of $300 coming in from the property every month. How much are you prepared to pay for the property to make $300 from it each month? Real estate is a pure number game. You have to consider plenty of deals before you zero down on one by working out your math. Even if you have a host of professionals helping and guiding you with these deals, do not avoid doing the math yourself. You may save yourself plenty of stress and heartache by closely analyzing the deal before taking any decision.

7. Negotiate like a boss

Once you've identified a property, mention your offer. How much are you willing to pay for it? Then, work out the type of financing plan you are keen on using. The real estate agent may guide you with all of this. One tip to negotiate more winning deals is giving the property sellers multiple options such as $330,000 with the entire furniture included or $300,000 without the furniture. You may or may not want the furniture but such options work at a psychological level.

When you give people the choice of picking between multiple options, they will go with one option instead of trying to choose between yes and no. You can keep negotiating with the other party until you both can come up with an agreement. If you can't work out an agreement that is suitable for you, start hunting for other deals. In the event that the deal does go through, you can move to the mutually accept the contract and move ahead.

8. Close the deal and manage your property

The final step involves closing the deal and managing your rental property. You may want to use the services of a licensed inspector to do a thorough inspection of the home for checking its ribs and bones. A majority of rental investors prefer doing all their paperwork using a title company. Once you finish the paperwork and get the keys, you have to effectively manage it. Hire the services of an expert and experienced property manager if you won't be able to handle the tenants and property management yourself.

The property manager will be fully in charge of the property maintenance as well as deal with your tenants. You still have to ensure that they are doing their job well and things are being looked after. Rental properties can give you plenty of passive income and financial freedom if you start building an empire resourcefully and judiciously.

Conclusion

Thank you for downloading my book.

Like everything we take up, there is a learning curve in building and running a successful passive income enterprise. Nothing that's worth having ever comes easily, does it?

Practice sound time management hacks and make the most of your multiple jobs or businesses. You may not want to quit your full-time job until you build a consistent, dependable, and steady passive income stream. The rewards of making tiny changes to your lifestyle on a temporary basis can be highly fulfilling in the long run. Think of it like this—you are giving your efforts, time, and money to earn your financial freedom in the future. You work for money now to get money to work for you later. Can it be any more rewarding than this?

If you truly enjoyed reading this book, please share your thoughts by writing a review would be greatly appreciated.

Social Media Marketing a Strategic Guide

Learn the Best Digital Advertising Approach & Strategies for Boosting Your Agency or Business with the Power of Facebook, Instagram, YouTube, Google SEO & More

By Sean Buttle

Table of Contents

Chapter Six: Building Passive Income with Udemy Courses

Chapter Seven: Get Rich Flipping Domains

Identifying and Scouting for Valuable Domains
Selling Domains

Chapter Eight: Slaying the Passive Income Game with Real Estate

Step-by-Step process for Rental Property Investment

Conclusion

Social Media Marketing a Strategic Guide

Table of Contents

Introduction

Chapter 1: The Importance of Social Media

Chapter 2: Which Social Media Platform Is the Best?

Chapter 3: Facebook – The King of Social Media

Chapter 4: The Visual Effects of Instagram

Chapter 5: Google and the Power of SEO

Chapter 6: The World of Twitter

Chapter 7: Can My Business Benefit From YouTube?

Chapter 8: Finishing Out with LinkedIn

Chapter 9: Applying This to Your Business

Conclusion

Introduction

Congratulations on downloading *Social Media Marketing a Strategic Guide* and thank you for doing so.

The following chapters will discuss everything that you need to know to finally get your social media plan off the ground. There are very few businesses who will succeed in our modern business world if they do not have a good marketing plan that includes some social media. Your customers are online, and they are looking for you there. If you are not present in the right places at the right times (and this includes on social media), then your customers are going to find someone who is.

This guidebook is going to spend some time looking through the steps that you need to take in order to work with social media and to gain the best results in the process. We will explore why social media is so important, before diving into all of the different social media sites that are out there, and how to use each one to your own benefit!

Inside, we will explore organic and paid advertising techniques, along with who should use, all of the major social media sites like Facebook, Instagram,

Google, Twitter, YouTube, LinkedIn, and more! While your marketing campaign may not include all of these all of the time, knowing how they work and who will benefit from them the most is going to make a big difference in how well you respond to them, and the results that you are going to be able to get in the process.

Now marketing campaign is complete without using some social media in there, and many companies choose to have two or three social media sites that they spend time with. There are so many things that you are able to do on these sites, and so many ways that you are able to interact and connect with your customers like never before. When you are ready to start increasing your own social media presence, and you are ready to really showcase your products and se your sales and business grow, make sure to check out this guidebook to learn how to get started!

There are plenty of books on this subject on the market, thanks again for choosing this one! Every effort was made to ensure it is full of as much useful information as possible, please enjoy!

Chapter 1: The Importance of Social Media

As a business, it is important to take a look at all of the different options you have available when it comes to advertising and getting your message out there. Not all of the avenues that are available are going to work for your specific needs. While there are many choices, some will work better for local businesses, some will work best for bigger companies, and some will work better for a variety of different reasons. Knowing your own target market, and having a good idea on who you would like to reach can really ensure that you don't waste your marketing money on campaigns that don't work for your needs.

One avenue that you may want to explore when it comes to your market campaign is social media. Social media is taking over the world, and no matter what kind of product you sell, it is likely that you will be able to find a good portion of your customers on one social media platform or another. And since there are so many options to pick from, and many of them are very affordable to advertise and market on, it is worth your time to check them out.

There are a lot of different benefits to adding at least a little social media to your marketing budget.

You will be able to reach more of your customers, can increase how much loyalty there is to your brand, and you can reach your customers were they actually are. Some of the other benefits that you are going to enjoy when you start with your own social media campaign includes:

Increased brand recognition

Every chance that you are able to syndicate the content that you want to use, and increase your visibility to the public is going to be valuable. Your social media networks, the ones that you choose to focus on for a bit, are just going to be new channels for the content and the voice of your brand. This is important because it is going to make you easier and more accessible for the customers while making you more recognizable and familiar to the customers you already have. Both of these are going to do wonders for helping your business grow to new heights.

For example, maybe you have a user who is on Twitter quite a bit and they hear about your company wen they stumble on it in a newsfeed. A customer who may be considered apathetic might become more familiar with your brand when they start to see it on several networks, rather than just occasionally on one.

More brand loyalty

According to one report that was recently published by Texas Tech University, brands who spend time being engaged on their various social media channels are going to enjoy a higher amount of loyalty from their customers. This means that, if you are able to, you need to take advantage of all the different tools that social media will give you when it is time to connect with your audience.

You may find that having an open and strategic kind of social media plan could be so important when it comes to morphing consumers to being loyal to your brand. If you find that you are struggling with getting people to not only try out your brand and your products, and to actually stick with you over the long term, then it is time to start a social media strategy if you don't have one, and improve one if you have a strategy in place.

More chances to convert your consumers

Every time you put a post on social media, it is going to present you with a chance to convert some of your customers. when you start to build up the following that you need on social media, you are, at the same time, gaining access to some new customers, some old customers, and some recent customers. And these posts allow you to interact with all of them. Every image, video, blog post, or comment that you share gives you another chance for someone to react. And each of these reactions could potentially lead to someone visiting your site and maybe even with them making a purchase.

Now, this doesn't mean that each and every interaction that occurs with your brand is going to be a conversion. But, every time that there is a positive interaction there, this means that the likelihood of them doing an eventual conversion goes up. Even if you notice that the rates of click through are pretty low, the sheer number of chances of meeting with customers, past, present or future, is going to be higher than anywhere else.

Increased traffic

Without the help of social media, the amount of inbound traffic that you are going to bring into your business is going to be limited down to just those who are familiar with the brand from other sources, and individuals who are searching for the keywords that you took the time to rank. Every social media account that you are able to add to this will mean that there is another path that goes back to your website, and every piece of content that you add to the social media profile means that it is going to give you a new opportunity for a brand new visitor to come and see your website.

Of course, you need to take some precautions with this. Just because you have a social media site doesn't mean that you are going to automatically get the new customers that you would like. You need to be willing and able to post content on a regular basis, keep the content high quality and consistent, and you need to interact in the right way with your customers. If you are able to bring all of these things together on your social media profile, then this means that you are going to be able to really see some great results with the amount of traffic that starts to head to your website.

Lower marketing costs

One of the things that you are going to love the most about social media marketing is that it can be really efficient, while decreasing the amount of costs that you pay to market your brand and products.

According to Hubspot, 84 percent of marketers found that they could spend only six hours each week on their social media accounts in order to see an increased amount of traffic.

When you think about the big picture, and how much you spend on the other marketing avenues that you choose to go with, six hours is not that much. You can spend just an hour a day doing this, coming up with a strategy and developing the content, and then you would start to see some of the results that come with your efforts.

Even when you are focusing more on paid advertising with Facebook and Twitter, your costs are going to stay pretty low. Both of these are going to be inexpensive, and you can have a lot of control over how much you spend on these based on your own goals. For example, many marketers start small to see how things go and to get a feel from the work, and then they build up from there based on how the trial run went.

Better rankings on a search engine

As many companies already know, SEO is going to be one of the best ways that you are able to capture the kind of traffic that you want from search engines. But the requirements that are needed to ensure that you are successful with SEO are always changing. It is no longer enough for a company to just update their blog, ensure optimized title tags, and meta descriptions.

Instead, you have to go through and add in a lot of other things as well. But the good news is that you can work with social media accounts and help to increase your rankings. Being active on your social media account, making sure that you interact with others, and producing some high quality content is often going to be a great way for you to really grow your presence online and to get the traffic that you want through SEO.

Better insights about your customers

And finally, the last benefit that we are going to talk about when it comes to social media is that it is going to help you gain some really valuable information about your customers, how they behave, and what they are the most interested in. for example, it is possible that you would go through all of the comments to figure out the way that others think and talk about your business.

Based on the information that you can gather on your customers through these social media sites, you may be able to segment them out based on topic and see which types of content seem to bring in the most interest, and then you will want to produce more of that content over time. You can measure the conversions that happen based on the different types of promotions that you try, and eventually, you are going to find the perfect combination to help you generate the revenue that you want.

As you can see, there are a lot of reasons that many businesses want to work with social media. It does not cost a lot of money for you to get started with this kind of campaign, and it is going to help you to best reach your customers where they are located at the time. When you are able to really work to come up with a good social media strategy, then you are going to be able to really see the growth that you want in your business and with your sales.

Chapter 2: Which Social Media Platform Is the Best?

The first question that you need to ask yourself is which of the social media platforms is going to be the best for your marketing needs. You may look at them and think they are all amazing and that you should spend time on each and every one. While they all have a lot of customers and a lot of things that are unique about them that will make them stand out from the crowd, remember that you do not need to advertise on each one. Your customers are not going to be found on each one, and spreading yourself this thin can be hard.

So, how are you supposed to know which ones are the best for you? This chapter is going to help you out with this by providing a brief overview of some of the most common social media sites that you can work with, how they work, and which kinds of businesses they are going to work the best with. For most customers, you will find that working with two or maybe three of these options is going to be enough. This will help you to use your money and time efficiently while still reaching as many customers as possible. Some of the best social media sites for you to consider will include:

Facebook

For many people, the number one social media site that they are going to use to help them market to their potential customers and earn more sales is through Facebook. Facebook is considered king when it comes to working online, and with billions of active users who spend several hours or more a day online, this is definitely a spot where you are going to find a lot of your potential customers as well.

While not every business is going to concentrate their efforts fully on Facebook, especially if they have a very niche market that seems to be present in another social media site, it is still a great place where you should spend at least a little bit of time. There are a lot of people found on Facebook, many options for advertising, and so much more.

We will get into how to market on Facebook a bit more later on, but you will find that it is a great option to help you earn a good amount of customers. you can use organic advertising and traditional paid advertising as well based on how you want to reach your customers, and so much more. Facebook is a place where you can find even your niche customers, which makes it the perfect option to help you no matter how big or small your audience is at the time.

Facebook is a great option to go with because there is just so much that you can work with. There is a large audience, and many companies have been able to grow their presence on there with just organic reach. This means that their marketing budget was low, outside of the person or team they hired to keep the social media site up and running.

If you already have a good presence online and your business has grown, then Facebook is going to be an easy place to start. A lot of your customers are already there, they are interested in learning about you, and some may already search for you online, making growing your reach easier than you can imagine. You still need to be present and make sure that you respond to them, post valuable content, and be consistent, but growing your following will be easier.

However, for those companies who are not large and well-known, the ones who are just getting started with themselves, much less their social media presence, there is still a lot of room for growth when it comes to Facebook. Both through organic reach and paid advertising, you will be able to reach the customers you want in no time. And since Facebook is such a large and growing network with customers based throughout the world, you are sure to be able to find the right customers for your needs, no matter how you decide to split up your target market.

Instagram

Instagram is the world of pictures and images. The majority of what you are going to see when you work on this social media site is a lot of pictures from companies and individuals all over the world. In fact, while you are able to add some ad copy and words to the pictures, the individual is going to be presented with the picture first, and then they have to go through and actually click on the image to see more.

If your business could really benefit from the use of images to showcase your work or your product, then you really need to work with Instagram as much as possible. Images are the rule when it comes to this social media site, and the higher quality, and the more creative you are able to make those images, the more you are going to get your potential customers interested in what you are doing and what you have available for sale.

In addition to working on the best pictures possible, it is also an option for you to use hashtags and other little additions to make it easier for your potential customers to find you. With some compelling copy, a good link in your bio (Instagram won't allow you to add the links to the individual pictures), working on a few relationships with the right people online, and the right hashtags so potential customers can find you, and you have the recipe for success on Instagram.

Instagram is going to work the best if you are looking to rely on a lot of imagery to sell your product or service. In fact, it is possible to have quite a few followers who won't even look at the words that you post on your site. They will be drawn in by the good visuals. Then, when they finally see something that they like, they may be enticed to push on your website link and check it out.

This doesn't mean that you should not spend some time on the copy that you add in. And the hashtag is going to be super important to make sure that new and existing followers and customers are able to find you when they need to. Having good and compelling copy with the right tags is going to help you so much. But the most important thing to focus on when you spend your marketing budget on Instagram is the imagery and the videos that you decide to post.

Google

Google is a great social media site for you to work on when you need to grow your SEO and help more people find you through search engine queries and more. There are a lot of times when your potential customers are going to find you online. They will put in some kind of keyword search online, and then if you match up with it, then this is going to get the to your website, helping you to get a good sale.

The better your SEO campaign and work, the more customers you are going to get to your website. And the more that you are able to get people to the website, the more potential sales that you are able to get. SEO is important for every kind of business, but if you rely a lot on your website traffic or another website like a blog, then the Google social media marketing is going to be the choice that you will want to spend your time with.

Many businesses are going to be able to see benefits when it comes to working on their SEO, so adding a bit of this to your work is going to make a big difference.

Even if you just put a small part of your budget towards this, it is going to give you some big results, and can really be enhanced when you are working with some of the other social media sites as well.

As you will see while we go through this guidebook, there are actually a lot of different things that you are able to do when it comes to working with Google. You will get the benefit of different features, search engine help, SEO, and more. Utilizing all of these doesn't have to be expensive, and this is why working with Google is going to help you to really get a good return on investment with it.

Twitter

Twitter is a unique social media site that you can choose to use. Many businesses are turned off from it because there is a character limit on it, which can make it more of a challenge to get your message across. But this is not done because Twitter wants to make your life difficult or doesn't care about how hard this makes things. It is done because they want to encourage more conversations and relationships and interaction, rather than letting people put up really long and boring posts.

It is tricky to get onto Twitter and do some good posting, but if your research has shown you that this is where your customers are located, then this is a good place to start. It will allow you to focus on giving a message that is clear and concise, and providing your customers with something of value, rather than just rambling on.

Remember that this is more of a conversation rather than you just talking down to the other person. If you are able to share interesting links and pictures and more with your customer, talk back and forth with them, and really focus on the keywords and more that you want to use when it comes to working with Twitter, then it is going to be easier to stick out from the crowd and get the results that you would like at the same time.

YouTube

YouTube is a great option to go with, especially if you are a business that is creative, and really wants to show off some of your skills in a more visual way. Many companies that do more service oriented options are going to like this because it gives them a chance to show off their expertise on the subject, since they don't really have pictures of their products to sell. This doesn't mean that YouTube can't work for a lot of different businesses. Too many times a company is going to miss out on all of the great things that they an do on YouTube because they don't think it is for them, or they think that it is going to be too hard to work with.

YouTube is a great place to get ahead of the competition, and really show off what you are able to do. There are many options with YouTube that are going to be great, and showcasing your business through video and other graphics can really be different, especially if you are able to do it in a way that is creative and new.

When you go on YouTube, you need to take some time and really think through what you would like to do. It is not enough to just decide that you want to create a vide. There are millions of videos uploaded to YouTube and so many hours devoted to watching the content that is there. This can be a good thing because it allows you to really find the customers you want to work with, but it also means that you need to be able to stick out and impress the people on there.

If you make a video that is boring and won't get anyone past the first few minutes, if not even less, then you are going to run into some troubles. No one will watch, you won't get any more conversions or traffic to your site, and your sales will stay stagnant. Of course, you may find that the opposite is true if you are able to work on some really high quality videos over time. The more unique and creative and high quality your videos, the easier it is going to be for you to convert some of those customers you want.

LinkedIn

The final place that we are going to look when it comes to finding the perfect social media platform to grow your business is the LinkedIn platform. When you spend some time marketing on LinkedIn, it is going to help you to better engage with a community of professionals that will help to drive the actions that you think are the most relevant for your business.

There are a lot of businesses and young professionals who will spend their time on LinkedIn, looking for jobs, looking for a way to network with other similar professionals along the way, and more. If you have a product or serving that you are able to give to either side of the spectrum then this may be the place where you need to start.

LinkedIn, is not always the first place that people are going to consider when it is time to look for a place to advertise themselves. This is often seen as a way to find new employees, to find a new job, or to network in other ways that can grow the business. But your business is going to be able to do the same things, and get the same benefits, if you just learn how to use this social media site to your advantage.

There are some kinds of businesses that are going to do really well with this kind of platform. And then there are those who need to go and pick out a different platform to spend their time because they are never going to see results with this one. For example, if you are trying to sell ice cream in a small town up north, there probably isn't going to be a lot that you will get out of marketing on this site.

If you are a company that sells business attire, it may be a good to advertise on here. Since there are a lot of young professionals on this this, including ones who want to be able to get ready for an important interview and look their very best. If this or another similar product are available to you, then working with LinkedIn may be a great option.

As you can see, there are a wide variety of different types of social media platforms that you are able to use in order to help you to get the best results with your social media marketing. But with all the choices, it is easy to get caught up and just want to start advertising with everyone, with no attention to what you are doing or whether it is a good idea or not. Learning how to distinguish from all of the different social media sites and learning which ones are going to be the best for your needs is the biggest trick to learn.

Chapter 3: Facebook – The King of Social Media

The first social media site that we are going to take a look at is Facebook. Everyone has heard about Facebook, and it is likely that you have your own personal profile on this website. But it is now time to brig your business onto this media site and spend some time promoting yourself there in full force, if you really want to bring in the customers. Let's take a look at some of the ways that you are able to work with Facebook and get the best results possible.

Market with your Facebook Page

The first tool that you need to work with on Facebook, and one that doesn't cost you any money at all, is using a Facebook Page. This is similar to a personal profile, and it is the hub of information about your brand, whether you are offering a service, a product, or information for your company. Users are able to Follow or Like your page, which allows them to receive updates that you post on their news feed.

If you do this method, remind your customer to go through and actually click on the option to view posts first. Facebook has changed some things, and if customers do not do this part, they are not going to see these updates without going directly to your page. This is because Facebook wants you to pay for this kind of visibility and reach. If you can get customers to click on "See First" you will be able to reach them in a more organic manner, which can save you a lot of money.

You won't be able to get all of your customers to do this of course, and there is nothing wrong with using some paid advertising to get results on Facebook, but why spend more money than you need to when it comes to working with your marketing budget? When you ask people to come and like your Facebook Page, ask them to recommend that they follow and see your posts first. This can save you a lot of money from boosting each post, and will keep your customers coming back for more over time.

The trick is to find people who are going to be interested in liking your page. You want to make sure that you are reaching them as much as possible, but if you don't have many people who are interested in following you from the start, it takes some time to get off the ground. We will look at some ways that you are able to get more followers to your page later on, but first, let's explore some of the things that you can do to help set up a great Facebook Page so you can draw more organic traffic to the area.

How to set up your Page

As a business, you want to make sure that you are using your Facebook Page to its full potential. At the very least, you want to make sure that you are not using the Page in a manner that is going to drive away your customers and ruin your credibility and business. The good news is there are a few steps that you are able to follow that will help you to really get the most out of your page and see the results that you want from Facebook.

First, we need to take a look at choosing the right cover image and profile picture. If you have a logo, this is probably going to be the best thing to put as your profile picture. This helps to keep things simple, and ensures that others are going to be able to see what you have to offer and current and potential customers will know they are at the right place.

The cover image can be a bit different thought. You can have some fun with this one based on the kind of business that you are trying to run. It is really going to be up to you what you would like to do here and you can get creative if you would like. Sometimes adding contact information, pictures of your business or employees, or even some fancy artwork can help with this. Just make sure that it is professional, appropriate, and that it fits with the business that you are trying to run.

Next we need to focus on the about section. This is going to be placed right beneath that logo. This is a chance to really talk your business up, and to tell anyone who comes to your page more about you. You don't need to fit in every little thing about yourself here though. Just talk about some of the basics of what your company does. You can save some more of the details for the full about section later.

If you are in a hurry, you can use the About page of your blog of website, or some up with something unique to help you stand out to your customers. You want to work with a casual tone, one that is going to be friendly and informal for your customers.

The information that you post on your timeline, such as the status updates, need to have some purpose behind them. You want to make sure that the information has some use to your fans. Don't always have endless updates about the same thing, and don't try to post too often. Some ideas of what you can post to your audience would include:

1. Links to some articles related to your industry or your company.
2. Links to any posts that you add to your blog.
3. Coupon codes that are exclusive to your Facebook fans to help them save on your products.
4. Any announcements about new products.
5. Links to any kind of online tool that you think your fans are going to find the most useful.

No matter what you decide to post, make sure that it is useful to your customers. If it is just to fill up space, then it is not worth your time to post on here. Having a lot of variety of content, and finding the best time, and number of times, to post will make a world of difference in the results that you are able to get with this as well.

How do you know if you are posting at the right time, or if you are posting information that your followers will find useful? Check your statistics and some of the results that you get from them. Facebook Insights is a great tool that you can use that will offer you some great analytics for your page. You need to pay special attention to them to see if there are any times with a big surge from the fans, or times when the fans seem to go down. You can then start to see some of the patterns, and use this to your advantage.

Ways to drive traffic

The most obvious answer that you are going to see when it comes to this one is that you would use paid advertising on Facebook in order to bring in the customers. And you can certainly use this method if you would like. But our goal here is to get the most out of Facebook, without having to spend too much on our marketing campaign and spending for every little thing. Luckily, there are a few things that you are able to do in order to set up your Page and get more viewers without having to spend a lot.

First, consider adding information about your social media platforms on your website. If you already have a good amount of customers who visit your blog or your website and make purchases, let them know that you now have a Facebook Page. Let them know that they are going to find useful information, deals, and more on the page. There needs to be some incentive on the page to help get people to visit there and use your page. Adding some posts with special discounts that only your Facebook followers can get can be a great way to get them in to at least look.

If you are already on other social media platforms, then alert them that they can follow you on Facebook as well. You want to make sure when you are doing this that there is some incentive to make it happen though. If you are posting the same information and the same deals on each site, then there really isn't much of a reason for them to follow you on both.

Doing promotions and contests can be a great way to get people to follow you. If you can convince your current followers to get their friends and family to follow you as well, then you will be able to get more and more people on board. Offering some incentive to share your information to encourage them to get talk you up can be a great way to grow your business. You can offer a big discount, give them free products, and more can really help.

And of course, you need to make sure that your posts and information are always high quality. If you are just writing to fill up space, or your content is not done on a consistent basis, it is going to be almost impossible for you to get the results that you would like. Your customers want to find something of value, and they don't want to be an afterthought with you. Make sure that you are posting on a schedule that works for you that is consistent, and you are going to be able to form a good relationship with them.

Working with paid advertising on Facebook.

Now, you may notice that above we are talking about some of the things that you are able to do to organically reach your customers on Facebook. These are the things that you should do in order to start getting your customers in, and to save money. You can do quite a bit of marketing organically, even if you do use some targeted advertising, to save money and reach your fans in new and exciting ways.

With that said, Facebook is going to offer you a fantastic targeted advertising platform. You are able to create some ads that will be targeted to certain ages, locations, levels of education, and even the type of device that they are using when they search your site. Facebook also lets the users hide ads they don't like or a Like page button right below the advertisement.

Due to the fact that Facebook is able to gather a ton of demographic information concerning the users on it, it is going to have one of the best targeted advertising programs that you can find. You can basically choose anything that you want to base your targeting on, and you can even track how much success you will have with each of the segments.

While this has gotten them in a bit of trouble recently, we're just going to take a look at how this is going to benefit you as a marketer. You are able to choose to run your ads based on a per-click or a per-impression idea. Facebook is going to show you what bids are for ads that are similar to yours, so you have a better idea of your bid is going to be similar to what others are doing in the industry like you. You can also spend some time setting limits for each day so you don't blow your budget.

The advantage of using this is that ads on Facebook are really powerful, and you will notice that they are going to be more likely to succeed than groups or pages since you are the one who can choose who sees the ad. Of course, you do need to monitor what the costs of these are going to be to help you get the most out of the campaign, without spending too much money.

The first thing that we need to take a look at here is the type of ad that you want to run. There are a few types of ads that you can choose. These can include carousel, canvas, leads, offers, and even video. Each of them are going to have advantages over the other, and it really depends on what you want to do with the advertisement and even what you are trying to promote at the time. Some of the advertisement types that you can work with on Facebook includes:

1. Multi-product ads: These are often called carousel ads as well. With these, you are able to advertise more than one product ta a time. As a marketer it is a good way to check the engagement among some of the products that you are listing.

2. Domain ads: These are the types of ads that are going to contain one image and then there is a description that shows up at the top and a link to your website on the bottom. These are often known as page link ads. They are the one that most advertisers are going to use on Facebook because they can be super effective.

3. Video ads: These are starting to really gain in popularity because it is a great way to influence various users you need to reach. While text can work well, videos are often much more effective at getting your message across, as long as you use them properly. They are often

going to be used for retargeting and for increasing the awareness of your brand.

4. Offer ads: This is the type of ad where you give the viewer some information about an offer that you have. these are going to be targeted mainly to your current customers. you want to target them with this deal in order to get users to go directly to your website with a unique code to hopefully get them to purchase from you.

5. Canvas ads: These are a great option to work with because it is more interactive. You are able to look at the tab for publishing tools on your page. Then you can create the interactive part that you would like.

6. Lead Ads These are going to look the same as the standard Facebook ads, but they are going to be focused on getting the information about the user that you want, without having to leave Facebook. You may be able to get some information like their name and their email address to use for more targeting later.

7. Branded content: These are going to be a type of sponsored ad. Often you are going to get together with another company or brand and then the two of you will post an ad together

with a tag. Both of you can benefit from the exposure and the lower price for marketing.

8. Dynamic ads: And finally there are the dynamic ads. These are going to be able to collect some information from your website and then will make ads to your viewers based on that. You are able to add any personalization that you want to the ads. These are the kind of ads that show up when a customer has visited your site, and maybe left something in their cart that they didn't purchase yet.

Once you have an idea of what kind of ad you would like to run, you can go through and create a new ad campaign. You have to be the person who is running the page, so you need to be the administrator. From there, you can head over to the Ad Manager. It is a complicated tool simply because it has a lot of different features, but you just need to focus on a few of them to get started.

Powerful options for targeting

You will quickly find that Facebook is going to have some of the most powerful options when it comes to targeting your users. You are able to target pretty much everything that is on the profile of your user.

You may start with location if that is the most important thing, and you get the option to specify by zip code, state, city, and more. This can be helpful if you are a local business. You can then mov eon to some of the demographics that are the most important to you such as their age, their education, where they work, their relationship status and more.

There are so many neat things that you are going to be able to do with this. For example, you may be able to do some targeting to figure out who has recently moved to the area. If you own a gym, for example, you could do some targeting and figure out who has just moved to that area and then make the advertisements for them.

You can target based on the interests the person has. This helps you to target towards people who may have interests that go for your business. You can target those who like a certain book if you would like, or target a private list of users if you have some email addresses that you have collected so far.

Customize your ads

And to finish this off, one of the biggest advantages that you are going to have to these targeted ads is that you are able to customize it and create the ads that work for a variety of demographic groups. Better-targeted ads are going to help you to get the best results.

For example, let's say you sell baseball equipment and you want to be able to target baseball fans. You may decide to create ads that are customized for different popular teams. You could create an ad that goes for Cubs fans, one that goes for Yankee fans, and one for Red Sox fans. Then you will have these specific ads shown to those who have already gone through and shown that they are interested in those teams.

There are so many things that you are going to be able to do when it comes to working with your marketing on Facebook. It is definitely a site that you need to spend some time on, but you do need to be careful. You want to make sure that you are using your budget as wisely and efficiently as possible. It is easy to spend a lot of money if you are not paying attention to what you are doing with your marketing. But if you pay attention and really learn how to leverage Facebook and do some of the organic work as well, you will be able to have an affordable and effective marketing campaign on Facebook.

Chapter 4: The Visual Effects of Instagram

It is definitely a good idea for your business to concentrate on working with the Instagram social media site. While Instagram may be younger, with fewer users, compared to the parent site of Facebook, but it is still a breakout social media site that you should spend some time on. You will be able to tell a visual story through a lot of different formats. And, if you are able to reach your target market in the proper manner, you will find that this can give you a huge return on investment compared to some of the other places you may choose to advertise.

Why would you want to work with Instagram? Because it is estimated to have 800 million active users each day. And it is likely that this amount is going to grow more and more throughout the years. People love the idea of being able to find the visual options that are on here, and it is a really unique way to showcase your business and your products.

This growth may be a little bit scary when you are first getting started, and you may be worried about some of the clutter that comes with it. Organically, you can make a start, but you may find that, like with your Facebook account, you are going to need to do a bit of paid advertising to help you stand out from the crowd. Let's look at some of the things that you are able to do in order to really get the most out of your marketing dollars and a great return on investment when you work with Instagram.

How to reach your audience organically on Instagram

The first thing that you need to focus on when it is time to bring in some of the great things that you can get out of Instagram will be reaching the audience in a more organic manner. This is going to help you to reach as many customers as you would like, without having to pay for paid advertising and wasting money on marketing.

While there is nothing wrong with working with paid advertising on Instagram, you do need to also work a bit on organically reaching your customers. And there are a few things that you are able to do to make this happen for you. Let's take a look at some of the best steps that you can take in order to really reach your target audience on Instagram.

There are a number of things that you are able to do to help organically grow your reach on Instagram and other sites along the way. Some of the techniques that are going to work well for most marketers, especially if you are using them the right way will include

Use the hash tags

While the image that you put up on your page is very important to the success of your Instagram campaign, hash tags are going to be one of the most important elements of your post. Captions can tell a story with the image, but the hash tag is going to get your image seen by those who may not be your current followers. When users on Instagram start to search for hashtags that are relevant in a specific industry, you want to make sure that your posts are one of the ones that show up. If they don't, then this means your competitors are there instead, and you are missing out.

There are going to be three main strategies that can be used for choosing hash tags. These include:

1. Use hash tags that are pretty popular, ones that have the best chance of getting search for. This may end up with a lot of competition, but it still increases your chances of being seen.

2. Use some hash tags that are less popular, but still highly relevant to the work that you want to do. These may drive fewer users to your posts, but the ones who do find you based on these hash tags are going to be more targeted.
3. Use hash tags that are often thought to attract new followers. Some of the good ones to go with include #follow #follow4follow and #followme.

No matter which of the three strategies you choose to go with, or even if you decide to do a little combination of each one, try to use at least on hash tag on each post. Even more hash tags can be better because it increases the amount of reach you are able to get on this site.

Find the right amount of posts a day

The next ting that we need to take a look at is the idea of how many times you should post on your page a day. This is a question that is going to come with a lot of debate. Each marketer is going to come with a different answer to this one, and it is going to depend on your product, and your customer base.

There is a lot of information and advice that is conflicting when it comes to how often you will need to post on Instagram. In the long run, you are the one who needs to pay attention to the information that you are given, and the statistics that you look at, and then decide what seems to work the best for your needs. Some people may be fine posting just once a day, and others are going to need to post several times a day.

According to research that has been done on the idea of posting on Instagram, which was able to monitor 55 different brands who use Instagram, it was found that most brands would post somewhere in about 1.5 times on average a day. What seems to be more notable here is that posting more often didn't necessary result in less or more engagement. It all depends on what seems to work for your business, your time, and your customers.

In the past, most marketers were told to be overly careful about not posting too much on their pages. You shouldn't go too crazy with this and post fifty times a day every day. But if you want to post a few extra times one day, it is not going to hurt your engagement that much. You may need to experiment a bit and see how many postings a day will work the best for you.

Remember the vibe that comes with your brand

If you are looking around on Instagram, you will find that the brands that seem to have the most success there are the ones who will look carefully at their images and their posts and ensure that these are going to contribute to the identity of their brand. All of these companies are going to come with an overarching theme that ensures that all the videos, images, and other things stick with the same theme.

This is such a good thing and you need to stick with it in your own advertising as well. It is going to help your customers feel like they can really get to know you and our company. And when they feel that they are able to connect with you, they are going to stick around and see what more they are able to glean from you.

This means that you are going to have to carefully consider all of the pictures and videos that you want to put up on your Instagram business account. There are too many companies that will post things without thinking, and then it makes their brand look like a mess. While you don't want to have every picture become a clone of each other, it is a good idea to really think through any of the posts that you put up before you get started.

Steps to make sure your profile is optimized

It really doesn't take that long of a time for you to go through and properly optimize the profile that you are using on Instagram, but it can definitely make a big difference on how many people will actually click on your site. It can also make a difference on how they view your brand. Some of the tips that you can follow to help optimize your profile includes:

- Make sure that the description and the images on your profile go well with the vibe that you want to see in your company.
- Make sure there is always a link present that goes back to your website. You could even consider setting up a landing page that is specific for your visitors from Instagram, or you can make changes to the link to help promote a current campaign or other content.
- Use the logo for the company somewhere in the profile. This lets your users know that this profile is the official one for your company.
- Consider adding at least one brand specific hash tag to your profile. This makes it easier

for your customers to know the profile belongs to you.

- If you are a local business, or have your own store, consider including your physical location into the profile as well.
- Make sure that if you have other social media profile that your images, and any other content, stay consistent throughout.

Growing your followers

If you do not take the time to grow up a good base of followers who are actively watching your posts and checking in with you on a regular basis, then all of the other things that you end up doing on this social media site are going to be worthless. The secret to growing your solid base properly is simple, but it does take some time and effort in order to see it happen.

The secret that we are going to follow on here is a natural engagement. When you naturally engage with your followers, you will find that they are more likely to stick around. What this means is that you need to respond to your customers, consistently post, keep the information engaging and prevalent to what you are doing, and more.

Now that we understand how this works, there are going to be a few different strategies that you are able to use in order to make sure this process works for you. Some of the strategies that can work when you want to grow your Instagram following include:

1. Remember that quality pictures and posts are always going to beat out quantity. If you have already started your account, make sure that you go through and edit it until only the very best is left. No one wants to follow you if all you have is thousands of pointless images that have nothing to do with your business.

2. Always have a good and relevant caption with your pictures. Asking a question within that caption can be a good way for you to increase your engagement.

3. Be consistent. Always remember who you are posting for, and remember why you are posting.

4. Use various tools like Piqura to see which images are leading you to the highest engagement, and then post more of them.

5. Engage on the photos that you most, and also on other profiles. As people start to see that you are interacting on a regular basis, they are going to start following you as well.

6. Make sure that if you are on Instagram, you should promote this account everywhere that you go. Promote it to other social media sites, on your physical marketing materials, and to your email subscribers.

The importance of being a follower

Unless you happen to be a big celebrity and go on Instagram, it is likely that you will have to do some work in order to get followers to pay attention to you and to even get people to follow you back in the first place. Not only should a business focus on following their followers back, but you need to take an active role in making and finding new people who will follow you.

This is sometimes hard. Just posting on your page is not going to be enough to bring in all of the people that you would like. You have to put in a little bit of legwork to see this happen. Some of the ways that you can work to find the right people you want to follow, an hopefully get them to follow you back will include:

1. Look around for the people you already know. When you are on your profile, head to the main page before clicking on the right hand corner of the top of the screen. From there you can tap

on Find Friends and see who is on your suggested user list, contact list, and friend list.

2. Search for similar companies, or other companies you already know and who may have some followers who would like your company as well. You are able to find these using the search bar function.

3. Find others that you may want to spend your time following. Instagram makes this easy with their own Search and Explore feature. You just need to click on the magnifying glass icon and then do a bit of scrolling to figure out who is most recommended for you.

4. Follow influencers in the industry that you are already in. The program known as keyhole is going to help you search for users and posts using the hashtag from before, and then you can go through all of the results looking at the number of likes found on the post.

5. Follow any of the users who are already following top influencers in your industry.

6. Search for hashtags that seem to go with your industry. This is a good way to help you do a bit of targeting on the users who are in your field or niche.

7. You can spend some time searching on Google as well. This helps you to find some of the most influential users in your industry.

Make sure your posts are engaging

One of the mistakes that you need to watch out for when you are working with Instagram is that you don't start to post the same type of content over and over again. Posting product shots and selfies may be something that you are used to working with, but it is also a good idea to mix up things a bit and then change the strategy. Try something new, or have a nice rotation of things that you would like to try along the way.

The neat thing with Instagram is that there are a lot of different options that you are able to choose from in order to help you mix up the content and to really make yourself stand out from the crowd. Some of the post ideas that you can try out to mix things up will include:

1. Photos that your users submit.
2. A day in the life shot that is going to show a bit of your personal life instead of just the business.

3. Holiday themed videos and images do well.
4. Some demos or tutorials that show the customer how to work with your product.
5. Simple image quotes on the picture or video. You are able to do this with the help of Canva.
6. Sneak peeks of any new product that is available for you to show your customers.
7. If you can, take some photos that are behind the scenes in your business to make the customer feel like they are getting information that others aren't.

Paid advertising on Instagram

Another option that you can work on is doing some paid advertising with Instagram. This allows you to reach for some of the customers who may not have been available for you in the past, and can even target your current customers to ensure that you are going to be able to make some of the sales that you would like to see.

When it comes to advertising with Instagram, there are a few different types of ads that you are able to work with. The most common types that you will want to spend your time on include:

1. Stories ads: These are the full-screen ads that will appear in between the stories of other users. This allows you to target your audience very specifically and makes it easier to reach a massive audience with that ad. You an add in filters, video effects, and even text to make the promotion more fun. And it is going to look and feel just like a normal post, allowing you to reach a bit audience without ruining the experience for the user. You can add in a call to action to get your audience to head back to your website or do another action that you want.

2. Photo ads: These are great for allowing a brand to really showcase their services and products with some compelling images. You can showcase some of your best products, and then add in a Shop Now call to action button before targeting who you would like the pictures to go to. Just like with the stories, these are going to look just like the regular posts that you have, which can make the experience better for your audience.

3. Video ads: If you are able to make a good video that is short (fifteen seconds), then this may be the ad choice for you. This can be creative and can quickly make its rounds with a good call to action if you set it up in the proper manner.

4. Carousel ads: These ads are going to give the user a chance to swipe through a series of videos or images, and then there will be a nice call to action button that can lead the customer back to your website. These ads are going to do a few things such as sharing a multi-part story, showing more than one product, and even dive deep into one product or service with up to ten videos or images.

While you are able to advertise your Instagram posts on Facebook as well, we are going to keep this simple and look at how you can do paid advertising on your Instagram account. If you notice that you have a certain post or type of post that seems to get a lot of engagement and you want to grow this, you will be able to promote it within this app.

First, make sure that you have a business account set up (which you should at this point), and then you can go right to the post that you would like to promote. Click on the Promote button. It is likely that you will need to log in with your account from Facebook to authenticate who you are. Once that is done, you need to be able to select your goal.

There are a few goals that you can have including driving more people to your website, making more sales, or even maximizing the number of users who will see your post. You can also add in a call to action button of your choice, choose the audience that you want for the post (or you can let Instagram do this for you), and then choose the ad duration and the budget. When everything is set up for you the way that you want, hit Create Promotion and see how things go!

You can always make adjustments to the advertisements that you are doing, and you can learn from what you are doing along the way. if you notice that one type of demographic is really working for your needs, then go ahead and start relying on that a bit more. If you look at the statistics and see that something is definitely not working, then it is fine to drop that and move on. Advertising on Instagram or one of the other sites will be a big experiment in trial and error and it is fine to keep trying things until they work for you.

Chapter 5: Google and the Power of SEO

The next thing that you are able to take a look at when it comes to your options in social media and network marketing is on Google. Google is going to utilize the power of SEO to help those who are searching for you, or searching for topics related to your business and what you sell, to actually find you. Being able to do SEO on Google, and on a few other search engines, is going to be the best way for you to reach your customers where they are.

There are a lot of benefits of advertising and putting at least part of your marketing budget to Google. This is never more true than when you are a business just starting out. Think of it this way; there are more than 100 billion searches done on Google each month. And it is likely that some of those are going to be your potential customers. Doesn't it make sense for you to make sure that your customers are able to find you when they do these searches?

When you take the time to go through the steps that are needed to create a good campaign on Google, it is going to help you learn an important part of the marketing process, if you haven't done so already, and that is to determine who your ideal customer is, how to target them the best, and how to invest in the right steps to actually get these customers in the door (or to your website).

Marketing on Google is the first place you want to start. This is a way that you are able to directly advertise to those who are looking for your product and service. Usually when they are doing a search on Google or another search engine, they are at least looking for quotes and ideas, but many times they are ready to make their purchase if they find what they want. This is the perfect time to get ahold of your customers. If you show up and are relevant to the search they were done, then you may be able to convert them into paying customers.

You can also work with a feature that is known as Google AdWords. This is a method that marketers are able to use in order to reach out to their ideal customers and offer them your business as an answer to what they are looking for when they search online. This can be a good way to moderate your costs because there is no minimum ad buy on it. As a smaller business, this may be a good place to start because it can save your budget and help you get your business up and running.

Organic advertising on Google

The first thing that we need to look at is some of the organic ways that you are able to grow on Google. Setting up some of these are going to help you to do a lot better when it is time to bring in some of the paid services that you want to use with Google. Keep in mind with this one, you are going to be able to use a lot of the tools with Google for free. For example, you can look through different keywords with Google AdWords or Google Keyword Planner in order to figure out which keywords will be able to help you set up your blogs and websites the proper manner.

When you are ready to work with organic reach on Google, you need to concentrate on your website, and maybe even consider a blog. You will be able to take a look at some of your products and figure out if there is a common string that you are able to stick with between all of the products. Then see if you are able to start a blog that will link back to your website.

You can then start to post a few well-done articles and blog posts on a regular basis to help you to reach your customers. For example, if you sell fitness equipment, you may want to write articles about the best time to workout, the different types of working out, the benefits of working out, proper nutrition, and more. These will help you to see the results that you want overall, and will make it easier to add in the right phrases and keywords to your website so that you can rank on SEO.

SEO is going to be more effective when you do some of the paid advertising options that are available through Google. But if you already have this set up well on your blog or website, and the works are done in the right manner (meaning that they are placed throughout nicely and the article is actually going to be valuable to the customer), then when you start to implement paid advertising with Google, things are really going to take off.

The different ways to advertise on Google

There are a lot of options that you can use when it is time to advertise on Google. Each marketer is going to have to look at the options and decide which of the options seems to be the best for them. Some marketers may find that working with AdWords and just using paid ads is going to be enough for them. Others may want to use some of the other tools that are available through Google and will include tools like YouTube, organic search marketing, Google Shopping, Google

Plus, and Google Maps to name a few. These take a bit more effort, but can ensure that you are able to find the customers that you need.

You will find that using several of the assets from Google in your campaign can really help you to get more out of your efforts, and will allow you to make adjustments to your strategy over time. These adjustments can be made based on what you see is working through the analytics and tools that are offered. There are a lot of options that you can choose to make sure that your business is optimized as much as possible through Google, and some of the top options to work with will include:

1. Google Play
2. Google News
3. Google My Business
4. Google +
5. Google Maps
6. YouTube
7. Google Search

You will find that working with the keyword planners and analytic tools are going to be another part that you need to focus on with advertising. These are so important because they help the marketer get the insight that they need to ensure they are always making the right choices each time. When you work with the Google Keyword Planner for example, you will be able to look up words you would like to rank in SEO and figure out the bids you should pay, whether they are good keywords or not, and more. These help you make sound decisions based on your business and what has been working for others in the industry.

Using the AdWords platform in Google

Although you do get some examples when it comes to working with Google in any marketing strategies, one of the easiest ways for beginners to start with this is setting up your AdWords account.

AdWords is going to be an advertising platform that Google offers to businesses to run ads on the search results page. With this option, a user or a marketer is able to spend some time researching phrases or individual terms, and then using them in their website to get themselves on results page. If you use this platform, there is also going to be an "ad" mark on your search result. When you use this kind of service, you are going to be able to bid on some of the keywords that you think your potential customers will type into the search bar when they are looking for your service or your product.

This can be important for you to grow your business. Depending on the keywords that you decide to use, it can get a bit expensive. But it does ensure that you are going to show up at the top of the search results when a potential customer is looking for your products or services. Since many customers do not want to search all day, they are likely to at least click on the first result they get, even if it is an ad. And if you actually picked out good search terms to use, and you are careful with creating a high quality website that your customers will enjoy, then you will be more likely to make the sale in the process!

This brings up another key point. Google is not going to just let anyone with a website do this and rank high for all the keywords they want. Google wants people to keep coming back and using them. So they do have a few guidelines and rules that you are going to have to follow. They are going to look through your website and check out the quality and the relevance of your account to determine whether your website can be ranked with certain keywords.

Google + Page for Business

In addition to working with the paid advertising that we just talked about, marketers are going to have the option to work with a feature from Google known as Google +. This is a kind of tool for social media that will make it easier for you to reach out directly to the customers you have.

Like with some of the other social media sites that we have talked about in this guidebook, Google Plus is a way for you to communicate and interact in a more direct manner with your customers while still making sure that the context of your brand and business are provided. Google + can also have a big impact on your search traffic volume and SEO compared to some of the other sites of social media, simply for the fact that it is connected to Google and some of the other options they provide.

If you go through and create your own business page with the help of Google My Business, you will find that you become a featured business in search results any time that a user is looking for local businesses. This puts you right at the top of the search engines, and can make it easier for the right potential customer to find you when they need you the most.

When you decide to set up this kind of business page using the tools that Google provides, you will automatically be setting up your own Google + page as well. When you are able to put both of these tools together, it is going to make it easier for your search results to go up. Plus, this page provides you with a social media presence so that you can easily communicate with your customers, answer questions, share important information, and really get out there and represent your brand.

Can I work with Google Maps in my marketing?

Any time that you set up your business page here, you can also use the feature that is known as Google Maps. This is useful to ensure that you show up, along with your location, any time that a potential customer searches for keywords that relate back to you. People who are looking for some of the local businesses that may be able to provide them with a certain service or product will be able to type in the keywords that they want before seeing your location on the map feature as well. This comes with your website or Google Plus page link, as long as you have done the right work and are ranked high enough to be in these results.

If you spend the time updating this Business page with information that is accurate and complete, this can help your rankings. Google will be better able to match your business with the searches that relate to it. Some of the things that you need to do to make this happen is add in the physical address, phone number, category of the business, and then verify the location, and you will be placed on Google Maps. The more detailed information that you are able to add about this, the easier it will be for you to show up in the right search engines, and for your potential customers to find you.

What is Google product listing ads

If you are working with a business that is going to sell some physical products rather than just working with a service, then you are able to work with the feature known as Google Shopping. This is a tool in marketing that will help you to increase your traffic quite a bit while also making sure that your revenues are going to see a boost.

Google Shopping is great because it will allow your users see your product show up in a product listing ad that includes the image of one of your products, the name of your store, sometimes reviews, and the price.

Try this out real quick. Type in some kind of item that you want to purchase, such as a new Fitbit. When you type this into Google, there are often some images with prices and company names that show up right along the top. This is because of Google Product listing ads. And if you decide to add this to your marketing campaign, your products could end up on the top of search results as well.

Google Shopping is going to be managed within AdWords, but you are able to set up a bid on your products, rather than specific keywords for a traditional text ad. Google is able to help you out here to ensure that you are choosing the keywords that are right for your products. This ensures that you are going to appear at the top whenever users type those words into the search results.

Product listing ads are a great thing to consider because they will ensure that you are going to get some more clicks from new potential customers, especially ones who aren't already familiar with your company and can become new customers. You will find that Google Shopping has really grown to become more popular as its comparison shopping revenue is going to keep on increasing, making it a very effective tool that you can add to your marketing plan.

Other Google Aps for advertising

For companies who are just getting started with the idea of cloud computing, you may want to work with Google Apps for Business, or G Suite, to help. This can streamline the whole process and ensures that you are able to keep everyone on the same page together all of the time. For G Suite, there are actually a few options available to you depending on your budget and how much you need to get done. For example, the lower end that allows you to just do the basics is going to be about $5 a month for each user.

There are a lot of different things that you are able to do with G Suite, so it may be worth your time to check it out. With this feature, you are able to verify the website for your business, and even set up your own email, one that all your employees are able to use, that includes your domain name. Think of the level of professionalism you are able to add if you have a business with its own email address. This can also help customers know who you are any time they read your emails or need to communicate with you.

This feature is also going to make your work and marketing a lot easier, especially when you are on the go. It can help you with email, shared calendars, and Google Drive. If you and your team are on the go quite a bit, these can help you to communicate and share information when it is needed. Using these business apps can speed up the process and ensures that you are as efficient as possible.

Working with the Analytics

Before we end our discussion on advertising with Google, we need to take a moment to explore some of the analytics that you are able to do with this site. You are going to end up wasting a lot of time, money, and resources if you just randomly use the features and have no idea what is working or not. Google Analytics can help with this because it can give you a ton of important statistics about your website while also providing you with the feedback that you need to know how the campaign is really working.

When you have started a campaign and let it go for a bit, you will be able to log into your profile and see how many visitors are heading to your website, where the visitors are located, where all of this traffic is coming from (is it through SEO, your blog, from other social media and so on), which tactics in marketing seem to be working the best, and how many of the visitors who come to your site are then converting into paying customers? You can even split it up and see how many customers or visitors are from PC's and how many are mobile users.

It is definitely worth your time to spend your efforts looking at the analytics on occasion and making any adjustments that are needed. You can use these analytics in order to track different aspects of your marketing campaign and see which ones seem to have the biggest impact when it comes to traffic to your website and highest conversion rates.

As a marketer, you may also use some of the other tools that are out there, such as Keyword Planner and Google Trends, to help you figure out the right keywords to use in various campaigns base don how many customers are using them and how well they are trending. You can then take those keywords and use them either in your organic search strategy, or in your AdWords campaign.

Keeping a close eye on your campaigns and learning what is working best and what you should avoid can be so important when it comes to helping you get the results that you want out of Google. Google has a ton of features that will help you to grow your business and will ensure that you can reach the customers that you want. It doesn't just rely on one platform, but a bunch of features that get the job done. And learning how to use it along with other social media options is going to make a difference in how fast your business is able to grow.

When you are looking around to see which social media sites you would like to use in order to make sure your business is going to really grow, you need to make sure that you add at least a bit of Google marketing to the mix. When this is added in, you are going to see some amazing results that will ensure your business is going to reach the new heights that you would like.

Chapter 6: The World of Twitter

The next social media site that we are going to look at is Twitter. With more than 313 million active users each month, and a demographic that is young too, Twitter can be a great place for you to market yourself and see some great results. And you will find that it is pretty easy to set up your own Twitter profit. You just need to come up with your own handle (the name of your profile), upload a good picture to be your profile picture, fill outa bio, and send out the first Tweet and you are ready to go. There are more steps to growing the account, but these simple steps will at least help you to get yourself started.

Growing a real following through Twitter can take some more work than just sending out Tweets when you have a big event or a new product. Twitter is useful because it helps you to engage with your audience and actually interact with them. This isn't going to happen if you just send out a few Tweets a year. Let's take a closer look at Twitter and how it can help you grow your business.

How is Twitter different from the rest?

The approach that you have to each social media site that you work with should be a bit difference. You won't be able to use the same strategy that you do with Twitter as you do with your Facebook marketing plan. It is important that you learn more about the way Twitter works and the best way to use it in order to get the best benefits.

There are many different ways that a business is able to utilize Twitter in order to reach their needs. Some of the main ways include:

- Managing their reputation
- Branding themselves
- Networking so they an find other similar businesses and potential customers in the industry
- Interacting with their customers, and potential customers.
- Driving engagement for some of the promotional activities that they are working on
- Sharing the content and information that they have about their business and about their products.

Just like with all of the other social media sites that we have talked about, most of these activities are going to have to do with interactions. It is not just about broadcasting out your content, like what can happen with Pinterest and Instagram sometimes. Twitter works because of open communication.

Now that we know a bit about the importance of Twitter and how businesses will often use it, it is time to go into some of the things that you need to know in order to get started with marketing on Twitter. We are going to go beyond the how to for setting up a good profile. We are going to look at some of the real strategies that will ensure you are able to reach your customers and that you won't waste your time through this platform.

What is Twitter Chats and how can I use it?

Many of those who are interested in working with Twitter are curious about the way they can gain followers While followers are important, you want to make sure that you have followers who are active rather than ones who just click on you and then never look at you again. The answer to this kind of problem on Twitter is going to be Twitter chats.

These are a feature of Twitter that have been around for some time, but there are a lot of marketers who are slow to trying them out and learning the power that comes with them. But as a new marketer on Twitter, you need to pay attention to these chats and see what they are able to do for you.

One of the main reasons that these chats are going to be so effective for you to use is because the ones who are on them are active followers on Twitter. Those on this feature are on Twitter and purposely there to interact, learn more, and try new things. These are the best followers because they are the ones who will talk back to you, reply to any of the Tweets that you put up, will Retweet your content and messages, and can even help you to get things started.

Now, there are going to be a variety of Twitter chat groups, so make sure that you do some research and find the ones that are specific to your personal industry. This will help you to really get the results that you want and will ensure that you will talk to others who are interested in your content and what you have to say. And remember, you can't just post an ad and run away. You need to be present, asking and answering questions, interacting, and finding ways to really add value for others who are already there.

Twitter video

While Twitter is not always the first option that people are going to think about when they want to get started with video marketing, this is still something that you can consider adding into your Twitter marketing campaign. Twitter may not be as advanced with video marketing as you will see with YouTube, but it does give you a few options that can be helpful when you want to promote using videos on this site.

The first option is to use the native video feature that is already available through Twitter. This feature is going to allow you to record videos that are up to 140 seconds long. When these videos are done, you are able to upload these straight to the stream on your Twitter profile. If you want to make things easier and your videos is going to be about two minutes or less, then this option can be a great one to choose. If you would like to do something a bit longer, or you would like some more features to use, then you may want to go with the second option.

Another option that you can go with when you use Twitter is Periscope. This is a live streaming app that Twitter actually owns. Periscope is able to integrate your content into Twitter, which means that if you do a live stream, this is going to show up on the Twitter feeds for your followers. Then, when the stream is over, that recording will still sit around so your viewers can watch it whenever is the most convenient for them.

The second option can be nice because you get the chance of going live. This attracts more attention from your potential customers because they can watch you, ask you questions, and so much more. Add in the fact that these Live videos were able to get more than 31 million views in 2016, and more as time has gone on, it is definitely worth your time to add at least a few of these videos onto your Twitter feed on occasion.

Paid advertising with the help of Twitter

There are a lot of different options that you can choose from when it comes to a Twitter ads. Some of the best options that you can choose from include:

Promoted Tweets

These types of tweets are simply tweets that you are going to pay to get displayed to people on Twitter who are not already following you. They can work just like regular Tweets in that others can comment on them, like them, and even Retweet them as they like. They will also look like regular Tweets in many cases, other than they will have a Promoted label on them.

These Tweets are going to appear on the users' timeline, or on their profile, near the top of search results, and even on the desktop and mobile apps for Twitter. This is a great way to discuss your brand and let new potential followers know more about you. If you are careful with the way that you set these up, and you make them really informative and valuable, it is likely that you will get a ton of interactions. The more interactions, the more people who will see the advertisement, and the easier it will be for you to get new followers.

Promoted accounts

Another option that you can work with is a promoted account. These are sometimes known as Followers campaign. Hey will make it easier for you to promote the account you are using for business to targeted users who aren't following you yet, but who may find some of your content interesting. This can be a great way to find people who are already interested in topics in your industry so they are more likely to start following you.

These accounts will show up on the timelines of those people you follow. They can also show up in the Who to Follow suggestions and search results. They will list out that they have been promoted, but they will also have a Follow button on them so your potential customers have a chance to click and start following your page.

Promoted trends

When you are taking a look at a topic on Twitter and you notice that it is trending, this means that there are a lot of people on the social media site who are talking about this kind of subject. This is also a hot topic that Twitter is sure to place on the timeline of many of their users, on the Twitter app, and on the Explore tab. If you are able to do a promoted trend, you can promote the hashtag of your choice and get this in the same place to increase your visibility overall.

Any time that one or more of the users on Twitter decide to click on the trend that you are promoting, they are going to be able to see an organic list of search results that have that have that specific tag in them as well. What shows up differently here, and is going to benefit you the most, is that with a Promoted Tweet, your business is going to be the first option that shows up on this list.

So, people will start to see this hashtag and may use it for some of the posts that they do as well. This helps you to gain a bit more organic exposure, and it is likely that people are going to see your business as the top result because of your promotion. This ensures that you are able to get the most reach possible for your campaign.

Working with the automated ads

And the final promotional method that you are able to use when you go on Twitter is to work with an automated ad. Twitter has a neat thing that is known as the Twitter Promote Mode, and it works really nicely for those who are not familiar or all that comfortable with marketing on social media yet, and who would like a bit of help.

If you go with this option, it will be around $99 a month to use it. When it is turned on, the first ten Tweets that are done in the day will be promoted automatically to the audience that you have selected, as long as they are a high quality target audience as determined by Twitter. Replies, Retweets, and quote Tweets will not be included in this. You will also be able to work with a campaign for a Promoted Account that is ongoing at all times.

Remember that if you do go with this one, you may have to go into it and make the necessary adjustments as needed. For example, you will need to take the time to write out the Tweets that should be used, you need to decide on the right audience for the ads to target, and more. However, if you are able to do this, it is estimated that this feature from Twitter will help you reach an additional 30,000 people and gain at least 30 new followers to your business, so it could be worth your time.

As you can see, there are a number of different benefits that come with working on Twitter. Twitter is a great way for you to promote your business and open up communication with your customers in a way that just isn't found with other sites. Rather than just posting information (although you are able to do this on occasion), you will spend time in conversations with your customers, interacting with them, and more. Twitter can be a great idea to implement into your marketing campaign to get the most out of reaching your customers.

Chapter 7: Can My Business Benefit From YouTube?

The next thing that we are going to take a look at is how you can use YouTube to help promote your business. This is not a traditional site that a lot of companies will look at. If they aren't into advertising or something creative like that, they assume that they are not going to be able to see any results if they chose to go with marketing on YouTube.

The truth is, anyone is able to see their business grow if they just learn how to use YouTube in the proper manner. There are a lot of different things that you can do in some of your videos, and sometimes it is just a matter of thinking about what your customers want, or even just thinking outside the box and seeing what you are able to come up with. Let's take a look at some of the things that you can do with your videos on YouTube, and how you can increase your reach, both organically and through paid advertising, on YouTube, no matter what kind of business you are.

Optimized videos to get more searches and clicks

It isn't a big secret. If you want to make sure that you are able to see some success on YouTube, then you need to make sure that your videos are all optimized to work well not only on YouTube, but also on Google. By adding in the right keyword sin the right places, such as in your descriptions, tags, and titles, you can make it so much easier for customers to find you when they do a search.

We need to start by looking at the title. According to Google, it is recommended that you use the keyword you want to focus on first, then the branding second. This helps it to be more friendly in an SEO sense. You could also add in a season and episode number, if you find that is relevant, but put these right at the end. Your goal with this title is to create a clear picture so the customer knows what they are going to see when they click there, while also maintaining your SEO so you are easier to find. Try to keep the title short and sweet and to the point as well.

Working with tags is another thing to consider here as well. These tags are pretty simple and they are just going to be the main keywords that are going to relate to that video you are creating, and will tell others what your video is all about. For the most part, it is believed that YouTube is going to concentrate mostly on the first few tags that you write out, so try to make those ones as good as possible, or have your most important keywords close to the front. Your aim is to use all of the 120 characters you are given, but make sure they are all relevant to your video for the best results.

The description is going to be next. You need to spend time on this one to ensure it is high quality and will garner the attention that you want. Include a call to action so the viewers know what you would like them to do when they are done watching the video. It can be something like asking them to visit your website or to watch one of your other videos depending on your goal. Remember that the first few sentences of this description are going to show up in search results, both on Google and YouTube, so make sure that you put a lot of value there.

There needs to be a thumbnail that comes with the video as well. This is the image that the user is going to see that comes with your video. Don't skimp on this; try to bring in a high quality one that is going to draw in your customer and will help them to choose your video over one of the others that are available. You want to do an image that is 1280 X 720 pixels. YouTube can also generate a thumbnail as well, or you an upload your own.

How to promote your videos as well as your YouTube channel

The next thing we need to look at when it comes to organic reach with your videos is the different methods of how you can promote your videos and your channels. There are three main ways to get more views for the videos that you are creating and adding to your channel. These three ways will include:

1. Getting a rank that is higher for YouTube or Google keyword searches.
2. Having a subscriber base on YouTube that is large
3. Promoting your channel and your videos through other web properties.

The previous section already took some time to discuss the best ways to optimize the videos that you are working on. Growing your channel on YouTube, and being able to promote these channels and videos on other web properties that you own will be the next, and sometimes the most challenging part, of this whole process. Some of the ways that you can help increase your views and subscribers to your videos includes:

1. Promote these videos and your YouTube channel on the other social media profiles. You should include some hash tags that are relevant on these posts so that you get even more reach.

2. Engage with your loyal fans. When you spend time looking through the Creator Dashboard, you will see which users are the most engage with the content you provide. You can consider involving these fans in some way to nurture some brand ambassador relationships later on.

3. Add a widget for YouTube on your blog: You can use a tool such as Tint to help you display a number of videos, these can be your own or someone else's, in a widget that goes right on your blog or website.

4. Collaborate with other business owners who run a complimentary niche: approach some other YouTubers and see if they are willing to promote your videos if you promote theirs. You can even consider co-branding videos in order to use them for both audiences.

5. Engage with your users, both on their videos and on yours: Social media is going to see the best results when you interact and engage with others users, but this doesn't mean that you should just stay on your own channel. Leave

comments that are well thought out on videos and respond to any comments left on yours. Remember, the more interactions you have with your videos, the higher you will rank in the search.

6. Share your videos on your email list: Direct the audience to your embedded videos on your site in order to increase your page views and your video views.

7. Embed the videos onto your blog or website: Add videos to existing posts on your blog, or you can even come up with new blog posts that are specifically there to promote your videos. This will help you to increase your video views, and increase your pageviews on the site.

Making your reach organic on YouTube can take some time and may not happen as quickly as you would like. But it is a great way to ensure that you are finding people who are truly interested in the content that you try to provide. There are also some paid options that you can choose to work with as well, but whether these are going to be as successful as the organic reach that we have just talked about, depends on your audience, on the products that you are trying to sell, and more.

Paid advertising on YouTube

You also have the option of doing paid advertising on YouTube to help you reach more potential customers. Plus, paid advertising is often going to be much faster than what you are able to do on your own organically. On the YouTube platform, you are able to turn any video that is already on your page into an ad, or you can create a video that you want to use specifically as an ad. With the right targeting of keywords, you can make sure that your video is one of the first ones that shows up in search results, and that it appears alongside other similar videos when your potential viewer is online.

Marketers on YouTube are going to have a few options that they can use when it comes to targeting and setting up their YouTube ads. You can target based on a variety of demographic factors like keywords, gender, age, location, and so on. You can even choose how big the ad is going to be. Many marketers like to go with the larger ads that are 850 by 250, though there are other options that you may want to experiment with a bit to see if they work for you.

If you want to make sure that your videos are getting a boost each time you put them online, or you want to really grow your following and your profits online, then advertising on YouTube is one of the best options for you. For a marketer who has never worked online or with YouTube, the options may seem overwhelming, but it is a great way for you to get more social reach and can help you to get off the ground.

There are a lot of marketing options that are available when you decide to work with YouTube, especially when you are doing paid advertising. YouTube ads are the most common ones that you are going to use. And these will just be a video of your choice. Of course, you should never just randomly put a video up. You need to go with one that is high quality, one that you think may go viral if possible (this is a hard thing to predict, but if you aim for a good video that is catchy, it could happen), and one that may get the viewers to head over to your channel to see what other videos they are able to purchase.

If you are able to make a good video, one that has a good hook in the beginning that will keep customers on the video rather than clicking away, you are going to increase the reach that you have online. This is going to help you get the results that you would like, and will ensure that your return on investment from running these ads is as high as possible.

What is TrueView

One neat feature that you are able to explore when it comes to advertising on YouTube is the idea of TrueView. This is something that you are likely to hear about pretty early on when you start marketing. This feature is basically a way that YouTube is able to create some commercials, commercials that look similar to the ones that you may see with other online television or streaming services. This is actually going to be a highly successful form of advertising with YouTube and one that you as a business should take full advantage of.

When you are looking into doing a TrueView ad, you will basically need to start out by creating a short video for something that you want to advertise for, whether it is your channel, your brand, a product, or something else. Your goal here in most cases is to get any potential customer who sees the ad to really learn some more about the company.

Then YouTube will take these videos and place them at the beginning of another video that is being monetized. There are a lot of individuals and even companies out there who post videos and then earn money when advertisers put their videos at the front, and sometimes in the middle, of those videos. This helps those individuals to make money online, and ensures that you are able to gain more viewers.

Now, for this to work, the video that you would like to post to needs to be monetized. This is why there are still some videos that show up on YouTube that have no commercials on them. If the poster doesn't monetize their videos, it means that they are not going to have any commercials show up, and they are also not going to earn any money from advertisers on the videos as well. This can help direct your search when it is time to figure out which videos you would like to post on or not.

TrueView is not the only way that you can work to advertise your company on YouTube though either. Another option is to work with InDisplay Ads. These kind of ads are going to show up as a thumbnail next to the video that a viewer is looking at during that time. sometimes these are going to look similar to the PPC ads that other social media sites will use, but they will also come with a little thumbnail of the business or the video as well. From here, the viewers are able to choose if they would like to click on these ads. These are a great option if you would like to be able to promote other videos that may be present on your channel at this time. These InDisplay ads are a good way to restart a campaign that is viral or to get started with having people watch a bunch of your videos at once.

There are a lot of different options that you can utilize when it comes to TrueView, and you can be a bit creative in order to stand out from the crowd. You will notice though that when you use some of these TrueView ads, you are not going to be billed in the same manner that you are for a regular AdWords ad that you would place with Google.

InStream ads are going to be billed on a cost per view format. This means that you are going to be charged any time that someone clicks on your ad and then stays there for a minimum of 30 seconds. If this happens, regardless of the conversion or not, then you will have to pay. If the viewer doesn't click on the ad, or they don't stay for the 30 seconds, then you won't have to pay for that.

Now, you really need to make sure that you are creating videos that are high quality and will keep the interest of your viewer until they get to the call to action and perform the action that you would like.

YouTube ads are not stuck. This means that your viewers are able to skip them after three seconds, both on a PC and their mobile device. If the video doesn't hold their interest, they are going to be able to skip past you without getting much of a chance to know much about you.

This does allow you to get yourself in front of other people more, and some viewers, if you made the video well and had a nice hook in the beginning, may remember you and head to your channel to check out more as well. But it means that the standards are high. If you just assume that any old videos is going to do the trick and you don't come up with something that is high quality and attention grabbing, then you are going to end up with a lot of people just skipping over the ads that you are creating.

The ads that we have talked about here are going to fall into the cost per view format so keep that in mind. What this means is that you are going to be charged any time that one of your potential customers clicks on the thumbnail of the video and watches it on their page. If the customer sees the add, and then doesn't actually click on it, then you won't be charged at that point. But any time a customer clicks, even if they don't end up finishing the video, you will be charged for that.

The above is the two main options that you are going to have when it is time to work with the option of paid advertising on YouTube. Having a good plan, and understanding how each works and whether they are going to be the best for you is so important when you are trying to set up a campaign that works for your needs. But the number one thing that you need to do, no matter if you are working on your organic reach or paid advertising, is the quality of your video.

People are not automatically going to see your business and then click on the link to make a purchase. You need to give them something to incentivize them to go there, a good video can be a good start. Show them about your company. Show them what you are able to offer. Or find something else that you are able to put into your videos to really impress them and convince them that it is worth their time to check you out. without this catchy video, and without any enticement to at least head over to your website, marketing on YouTube is going to be worthless for you.

Chapter 8: Finishing Out with LinkedIn

The final social media site that we are going to spend some time on now is LinkedIn. This is not a traditional social media site that you may consider. Known as being a place for young professionals to meet, and maybe even find their first job out of college, it seems like it may not be the best place to find those who would want to purchase your products. However, if you are able to use LinkedIn correctly, and you have the right kind of products or services, it can be a really successful way for you to earn an income and increase your revenues and sales in no time.

LinkedIn is going to be a great way for you to promote your own business. In fact, there are a lot of different benefits of using this and some of the top ones that will affect your business (and why you should consider marketing on this social media site) will include:

1. It is estimated that there are at least 65 million business professionals on this site. These professionals are not only from the United States, but from the whole world.
2. The average member on LinkedIn has an average annual household income of $109,000.

This is way above the average for most families, meaning that they have some disposable income, for the right products.

3. It is estimated that one person is going to create a LinkedIn login every second. This means that your market is going to grow over time, helping you to reach more and more people too.

4. Nearly half of the members on LinkedIn are going to have the authority to make decisions for their companies. If you are able to interact with them and reach them at the right times, that could be very beneficial for you.

If your business is looking to grow through mentorship, referrals, and networking, then it is easy to see why you would want to spend some time on LinkedIn. Like some of the other forms of marketing online that we have taken a look at, marketing a small business is going to be inexpensive on LinkedIn (you can even set up the profile for free), and it is extremely effective.

How to get started with the marketing

Now that we have an idea of the benefits of LinkedIn and some of the reasons why your business would benefit from using it, it is time for use to learn some of the steps that you are able to work on in order to see the most success with LinkedIn.

The first steps that you need to work on to see the most results with LinkedIn is to make sure that you create your own login, if you aren't already one of the members on there. you should also spend some time on the profile. You want to use the right keywords and the right information in order to make sure that others know how your business is able to help them. Your goal here is to make sure your profile pops out and can attract more customers to you.

Unless you are working your business as a freelancer, then it may be a good idea to create a company page on LinkedIn for the business. You will be able to set up that profile as a new business page as you work on the resume part of your profile. Your company page can then be linked in from the resume that you put on your profile. With these basics for your LinkedIn profile in place, you can start to market your business to others who are on this social media site.

Advertising on LinkedIn

There are going to be two ways that you can decide to dive into promotions and advertising on LinkedIn. You can choose to go with either the proactive action or the passive approach. No matter which approach you decide to go with, the more time and the more effort that you decide to put into your marketing efforts on this social media site, the bigger the rewards are going to be.

So, first we are going to take a look at some of the things that you would like to do with passive marketing on LinkedIn. Simply creating your own profile, working on some connections, and ensuring that you keep your account updated could be enough to help you get the attention of partners, influencers, customers, and clients you would like to work with.

This sometimes seems too easy to be true. But it can actually provide you with a number of benefits in the process. Some of the benefits that you are going to be able to get by doing the passive marketing method is going to include:

1. Helps you to gain some exposure to people who are looking for your services or products. The search feature on this site will allow others

users to find you when they are looking for the products and services that you offer.

2. Getting you to find potential customers. Your business connections on this site are going to help you get "in" with the businesses and people you need, many of whom you may not be able to reach in other methods.

3. Displaying your recommendations when others give them on the site. Recommendations are basically word of mouth testimonials for your business and for you. They are going to prove how credible you are and they will encourage people to do business with you.

The next thing that you need to focus on here is going to be the more proactive marketing techniques. Like most of the other tactics that you are able to use when on this site, the more active you are, the faster and more effective the results are going to be. There are a few steps that you are able to work with to bring in more customers as well.

First, make sure that you are posting updates on a regular basis. Make sure that your customers are up to date on what you want to work with and what you are going to do in the future. Include updates that are going to be of the most interest for potential customers and clients. Focus on how what you are doing will be able to help your customers achieve their goals.

Next, spend some time participating in groups. You want to pick the right groups though. Pick out ones that are going to be within your own interest and business. Discussion participation is going to get others to see you as an expert in your field. Of course, don't go on thee groups and then start to spam others all of the time. Make sure that you are there adding in value. Answer questions of your customers, do posts that are going to add value, and only add in your business when it is there.

While you are on this site, make sure to send out invitations and messages to those who are in your network, as well as to those who are in the groups that you belong. Again, you don't want to become a spammer or pester others. Your goal is to create the right connections, and the best way to do this is to make it beneficial to the other person and to you.

As you are doing all of this, you want to make sure that you look into some of the options that come with advertising and an upgraded, paid membership on this site. This is going to give you some more benefits that will help you to grow your business more, and more contact options as well. And advertising on LinkedIn is still seen as a great bargain while still growing your business quickly.

Creating a LinkedIn Ad campaign

Now that we have looked at some of the different things that you are able to do with your account, it is time to learn how to create your own ad campaign. To get started with this kind of campaign, you will need to have a few things including a video if you would like, some ad copy, a good understanding of the audience that you want to work with, and your own profile.

Once you are ready, you need to go to your login page and the LinkedIn Ads part. Then click on Get Started. You will then be able to see two different types of options for the campaigns that you are able to run including Create an ad, and Sponsor an Update. We are going to take a look at doing the ad, but if you think the other kind will help, you can do that one as well.

So, first we need to take a look at creating your ad. There are going to be a few different areas that you need to fill in before you are able to make this work well for your needs. Some of the information that you should fill out to get the most out of your ads will include:

1. Campaign name. You need to come up with a name that you would like to come up with for your campaign. This can keep things organized and makes it easier to find the information that you need.

2. Ad language; You are able to choose from a few options when it comes to the language that you want for your ad. Make sure to list this out to help you get started.

3. Media type: You are able to choose a traditional advertisement and all of its format, or you can go with a video that is going to include a button to start the video on the image.

4. Ad destination: This is going to allow you to add in some kind of link to the advertisement. You can link back to your profile page, or another URL based on your needs. If you are trying to drive traffic to the business website, for example, then you will want to add that URL in there to get people to click on the ad and hopefully get some revenues in the process.

5. Ad design: Now you need to work on the design when it comes to your ad. You want to create a headline and a description. The headline is going to be limited to just 25 characters and your description is 75 characters. Make both short and sweet to get the point across.

6. Ad variations: One of the neat things that you are able to do with LinkedIn is that you can choose from more than one variation for the ads that you want to make. You can choose to add your profile or an external URL. You can choose where you would like it to be located.

   a. Keep in mind that when you are working on LinkedIn, you are working with push advertising rather than pull. What this means is that the audience you are searching for is not really looking for the product you have. this means that you need to be able to make advertisements that will really stand out to people and catch their attention.

The next thing that you need to focus on here is targeting. You need to tell LinkedIn where you would like them to send the ads. Do you have a specific audience in mind. If you don't know about your audience, then it is time to do some research and figure out which group of people you would like to spend your time sending the ad to.

LinkedIn, like the other social media profiles, will allow you to work with a lot of options when it comes to targeting. You can choose your audience based on their gender, their age, where they work, their interests, their family life, where they live, and more. You can add in any kind of targeting that you would like to the mix to help you reach just the right person that you would like.

Before you send the ad out to the world on this site, make sure that you set up the budget that you would like to work with. You need to make sure that you are telling the site how much you are willing to spend for the campaign. You can choose a daily amount that you are comfortable with, or even a whole campaign amount, and let the site know. Think about how much reach you would like to have, and then figure out the budget that works the best to go with this.

LinkedIn may not be the option that a lot of people will think about when it comes to marketing their business. But there are millions of users on this site, and it is a great place for you to really reach the customers that you need, even before they know that they need your product. Doing a bit of organic work and some paid advertising will ensure that you will be able to reach the customers that you need.

\

Chapter 9: Applying This to Your Business

Now that we have had some time to look at the different types of social media and how they are going to work together, it is time to learn some of the things that you can do to ensure that you can grow your business with social media. You need to make sure that you are able to really take some of the benefits and neat features that come with social media, and implement it into your business, without changing up the way that you provide quality service and more. Some of the things that you can do to ensure that you are properly applying social media to your business, no matter what kind of business it is, includes

Set your goals for social media

Before you ever go to any of the social media sites that we have talked about above, you need to make sure that you have been able to set up some goals for what you want to get out of them. If you just come into it all without a plan and you only start posting random things at random times, and never communicating with your potential customers when they say something or ask a question, then you are gong to end up alienating others, and wasting your time and money.

Having some clear set goals are going to be the best way that you prepare for working on these social media sites. You will know what to post, when to post, how to interact and meet with your customers, and more. This ensures that all of your advertising on these sites, whether it is organic or paid, is going to be as successful as possible.

Always be consistent

You are not going to get the customers that you want if you are not able to stay consistent on the ways that you post online. Your customers are going to get pretty tired of waiting around for your posts if it has been a couple weeks or longer. And it doesn't work to post a bunch one day, and then not post again until a week later, and then have a few good days, and then go silent. There needs to be some consistency to what you are doing if you want any chance of catching the interest of your customers, and keeping it.

When it comes to the posts that you put up, the message that you are sending out, and how often you are on social media, you need to be consistent the whole time. this is truly one of the number one things that will determine if you are actually successful with social media or not.

Your goal here is to make a plan for this. Think ahead to what you would like to post, and how often you would like to do the posting, and then stick with this. It is ideal if you are able to post a few times a day to keep people interested in you, but you have to depend on your goals and your following. But you are not able to go from a schedule of posting once a month and then posting five times a day and then go back to once a month and then wonder why you don't have a following that is engaged in you.

If it is needed, consider sitting down at the beginning of the week, or maybe for a few weeks in advance, and figure out your posting. There are even tools that you are able to work with in order to do the posts for you. You can then list it all out with the content and the times, and then let the app do the posting for you, ensuring that you stay engaged with your customers, and you don't get off your schedule.

Consider the social media site that you want to use

You may find that one social media site works for one company, but it just isn't working for you. And maybe there are those who seem to be on all of the social media sites at once and can keep up with it all, and the thought seems to make you exhausted. The nice thing about this is that you don't need to follow what has worked for others. You need to find what is going to work the best for your needs.

Experiment a bit here and find out where your audience is, and where you are able to serve them best. Yes, everyone can benefit from bringing their business online and using social media. But that doesn't mean that you need to be everywhere all of the time. In fact, you may find that it is best if you are able to stick with about two or three that seems to work the best for you. This allows you to really concentrate on the information that you are posting, and ensures that you can really pay attention to what you are doing there.

In addition, learn to push on the networks that work the best for you. There are going to be some networks that seem to work the best for you compared to the others. When you find that there is a network that seems to work the best for your business, or for the customer that you have, then it is time to push on that network and try to take advantage of that one as much as possible. Take a look at some of the analytics that are available with it, and then change your marketing campaign to fit with that.

Make sure your content is best for each platform.

If you have more than one social media site that you want to work with, make sure that you are careful with the content that you are working with. Maintaining accounts on all of these is going to take some time, and you do not want to post the exact same images, posts, and more on all of them. You have to put in the work to format some content that is meant specifically for each platform that you are on.

For example, if you are working with Instagram, you are going to focus on the pictures, images, and videos to bring the customers in. LinkedIn is going to do better with some longer posts. Memes and videos are going to be great for Facebook. And when it comes to Twitter, you need to work with snappy and short announcements. All of these posts need to be different, even if you happen to be delivering the same message each time.

Double check that your message and content align

The next thing that we need to focus on is making sure that any and all content that you put on social media are going to align with the message you want to send out, the message that comes with your business. It is fine to share something that you find interesting or fun on occasion. But if you are just posting random things all the time, you may stray from your business message too much, confuse your customers, and defeat what you are trying to do on social media.

When it is time to build up your presence on social media, getting follows and likes is going to be a great thing. However, you have to look past the number of responses that you are able to get with your posts. There is a lot of temptation out there for you to just put up posts that get attention, but if no one is working with it and clicking on it, and if it isn't aligning with the message that you want to get out there, then it really isn't doing its job.

If you struggle with this, then it is time to bring someone in who can work on this with you. See if you are able to find someone who can look over your content and double check that it is lining up the way that you want. If the business is bigger, then there should already be someone there to help you with this. If you are the only person running it, then it is time to find a trusted friend or family member, or someone you hire out, who is able to do this for you.

Sometimes, your important content is not going to be that popular

It is tempting to only post up things that get a lot of popularity, or those things you know your customers are going to love. But then there are times when you will need to go through and make sure that you post information that is important, even though it may not be that popular.

You will find that there will sometimes be content that is automatically not going to get you a lot of shares and likes. These may include things like important blog posts, press features, charity posts, and testimonials. These are still important content pieces that need to show up. Without these, you will find that it is really hard to establish the validity that your business has in the market.

Despite how important they are, they are not going to help you get a lot of popularity points, and they don't get a ton of attention. This doesn't mean that you should give up posting it. Yes, these may not be the most popular posts that you put up, but they are going to be the foundation that you need to get your company growing and off the ground.

Learn how to balance your business and popularity

Your professional social media site is meant to be for your business, to help others find out about it and really help it to grow. This is why you need to post some of those things that are not that popular. However, this doesn't mean that you don't need to work on posts in order to get the attention that you want. It is fine to work a bit on getting some popularity, because this gets you the attention, shares, and more, that you need to grow your base.

Simply put, there is nothing wrong with being popular on your own social media site. This can be confusing, but you do need to make sure that you have a good balance in there between growing your business and really looking professional, and making sure that you are popular. You need to have a little bit of both and mix the more fun side that wants to be popular with the side that is informative and serious and is able to boost how reputable your business is overall.

Don't forget some of the organic work to help you.

While we did spend a lot of time talking about all of the great things that you are able to do when it comes to paid advertising on a wide variety of social media platforms, it is also important to work on your organic reach as well. While the organic reach doesn't seem to be as efficient as the paid advertising, you need to spend some time on it. This looks more natural to your customers, and it is going to really make the paid advertising more effective.

There are a lot of different things that you are able to do in order to help you get the organic reach that you are looking for. You can post on a consistent basis, you can make sure that the posts that you are using need to provide a lot of value to your customers, you need to use high quality pictures with your posts (no matter which social media site you are on), and you need to make sure to interact and communicate with your followers. This means that if you have a follower who is commenting on your posts or someone who messages you, you need to make sure to respond back to them in a timely manner.

When you spend this time working on building a relationship with your customers, it is so much easier for you to work with the paid advertising that you want. You will already have a nice relationship with your customers, and that will ensure that your paid advertising budget goes so much further overall.

How your target audience can help you choose the right social media sites

Your target audience is going to be so important with each type of marketing that you do. And it is especially important when you are working on social media. Without this, you are going to waste a lot of time and money trying to figure out which sites to go on, what kind of ads to do, and even how to target the ads that you are using.

Before you even think about joining a social media site, it is a good idea to think through the target audience that you have. hopefully you have been able to do this right from the start, but if not, then it is time to do it now. Think about the perfect customer. If you were able to walk into a large group of people and pick anyone to be your customers, who would that person be. Where would they live, what would they look like, what are some of their interests, their age, their marital life, their education and more.

Figuring out the answers to these questions will ensure that you are able to find the results that you want in the long run. Once you have a good target audience set up, you will be able to go through and pick out the social media site that is going to work the best for you. It also becomes a lot easier to know how to market to them, what kinds of advertisements you need to work with, and more.

Use those analytics

All of the social media sites that are out there are going to offer you some form of analytics. You will have to look at each of them on their own in order to figure things out, but it is still an important thing to spend your time and attention on. This can help you know more about your customers, learn where to find them, and figure out what is working and what isn't with your social media marketing campaign.

You need to check up on these analytics on a regular basis. These are going to show you what works and what doesn't. There are a lot of different options out you can do with each of the social media sites, but not all of them are going to work the best for your needs. Having a good idea of what will work for you, and what doesn't, is exactly what you want to look for when you research your analytics.

In the beginning, you may start out with trying a little bit of everything. This is not a bad thing to do. It allows you to spread out your budget and see what works and what doesn't. If you just put your money towards one thing, and not anything else, and that option doesn't work, then it could be a lot of wasted money along the way. Being able to spread out your budget against a few different options is going to make a big difference.

Once you have a chance to try out a few different options, it is time to check them out. the analytics will allow you to figure out what is working, what may need some adjustments, and what you need to avoid completely because it isn't working for your business or your customers. You need to make sure to do this with each social media site. You may find that something works on one of those sites, and it doesn't work on the other. It all depends on the audience that you are reaching in each part. Having this knowledge and putting it to good use for your needs will make your budgeting for marketing a lot easier.

Social media can be beneficial for each business, but there isn't a one size fits all when it comes to this either. Being able to put it all together, and learning what works and doesn't work for you, is going to be the trick that you need to really get the results that you want. Follow the tips above, and learn how to advertise and market in all of the different options that we talked about throughout this guidebook, and you will be able to get the most out of your social media marketing.

Conclusion

Thank for making it through to the end of *Social Media Marketing and Strategic Guide*, let's hope it was informative and able to provide you with all of the tools you need to achieve your goals whatever they may be.

The next step is to decide where you would like to work on social media. Trying to hit all of the platforms that we talked about above is going to seem overwhelming, and for the most part, it is not necessary. There is usually just a few of those platforms that you will be able to reach your customers through, and you will not need to go further than that. By now, you should have a good idea of the two main, maybe three, social media platforms that are the most interesting and helpful to you, and then move on to starting from there.

This guidebook has provided you with the information that you need to get started on social media and seeing the results that you would like. We looked at how to get onto the accounts, how to do some organic reach that won't cost you anything and can be very powerful, even with all of the noise online, if you do them in the proper manner, and even some of the steps to doing paid advertising as well.

Now that you are prepared and understand the importance of social media and the steps that you need to take in order to get started with your own marketing campaign, make sure that you get started with the help of this guidebook today!

Finally, if you found this book useful in any way, a review is always appreciated!